The Grammar of Fantasy

THE GRAMMAR OF FANTASY

An Introduction to the Art of Inventing Stories

§

Gianni Rodari

Translated and with an Introduction by Jack Zipes

§

Teachers & Writers Collaborative
New York

The Grammar of Fantasy

(Original Italian title: Grammatica della fantasia)

Italian edition copyright © 1973 by Giulio Einaudi editore s.p.a., Torino
Translation and introduction copyright © 1996 by Jack Zipes
Foreword copyright © 1996 by Herbert R. Kohl

Dedication

This book is dedicated to the city of Reggio Emilia.

Acknowledgment

The Grammar of Fantasy is published by arrangement with Giulio Einaudi editore s.p.a., Turin.

Library of Congress Cataloging-in-Publication Data

Rodari, Gianni.
    [Grammatica della fantasia. English]
    The grammar of fantasy : an introduction to the art of inventing stories / by Gianni Rodari ; translated and with an introduction by Jack Zipes.
        p.   cm.
    Includes bibliographical references.
    ISBN 0-915924-50-1 (hc : alk. paper). -- ISBN 0-915924-51-X (paper : alk. paper)
    1. Storytelling. 2. Creative thinking. I. Zipes, Jack David.
  II. Title
  LB1042.R6213 1996
  372.64'2-dc20
                                            96-11781
  CIP

Teachers & Writers Collaborative, 5 Union Square West, New York, N.Y. 10003-3306

Teachers & Writers programs are made possible, in part, through support from the National Endowment for the Arts. Teachers & Writers Collaborative receives support for its programs from the New York State Council on the Arts and the New York City Department of Cultural Affairs.

T&W also thanks the following foundations, corporations, and agencies: American Stock Exchange, Apple Computers, Bertelsmann USA, The Bingham Trust, Bronx City Council, The Bydale Foundation, Chemical Bank, Consolidated Edison, Charles E. Culpeper Foundation, Aaron Diamond Foundation, Heckscher Foundation for Children, The Joelson Foundation, J. M. Kaplan Fund, Lannan Foundation, M&O Foundation, Morgan Stanley Foundation, Network for Social Change, New York Times Company Foundation, Henry Nias Foundation, NYNEX Corporation, Prudential Foundation, Queens City Council, Helena Rubinstein Foundation, The Scherman Foundation, Schieffelin & Somerset Company, Variety–The Children's Charity, The Lila Wallace-Reader's Digest Fund, and two anonymous benefactors. Many thanks also to Gioacchino Lanza Tomasi and Paola Mignone of the Istituto Italiano de Cultura.

Cover and page design: Christopher Edgar
Frontispiece and back cover art by Jean-Ignace-Isidore Grandville
Printed by Philmark Lithographics, New York, N.Y.

Contents

Foreword

by Herbert Kohl

What is the place of the imagination in education? The word *imagination* does not appear in the government's list of "Goals 2000," nor does it turn up on lists of behavioral objectives or educational outcomes. There is no imagination curriculum or pedagogy of the imagination in our schools. Yet if, as the poet Wallace Stevens wrote, "the imagination is the power of the mind over the possibilities of things," then to neglect the imagination is also to impoverish children's worlds and to narrow their hopes.

"The possibilities of things"—the counterfactual world of supposings and imaginings—make it possible for children to stretch themselves beyond their everyday realities and confront experience with the question "What if?" What if there were no money in the world? What if you could change the meanings of words? What if you had a magic wand, a sack filled with presents, or the Holy Grail? What if people were made of butter, glass, or carbon paper?

Enter Gianni Rodari, stage left, with questions like these and with his grammar of the imagination. In this book Rodari examines the ways in which people—parents and poets as well as teachers and children—can collaborate in imaginative play. The word *collaborate* is the operative one. For Rodari the teacher is an "animator," someone who brings to life creative play across all subjects of the curriculum and all realms of the imagination. He envisions the teacher as "an adult who is with the children to express the best in himself or herself, to develop his or her own creative inclination, imagination, and constructive commitment."

The imaginative exercises in this book and the new role of the teacher were tested and eventually instituted as the core of teaching young children in the schools of Reggio Emilia in northern Italy. The goal of this work was to mold schools into cooperative, imaginative learning communities in which teachers and children engage in the imaginative exploration of reality—that is, in the exploration of what might be as well as what is. In such a context there is no hierarchy of fields whatsoever. Basically there is only one field—reality, encountered from all points of view, beginning with the first reality of the school community, togetherness, the way of being and working together. In a school of this kind the child is no longer a "consumer" of culture and values, but a creator and producer of values and culture.

This educational vision for young children is close to Paolo Freire's vision of adult education, and is one that fits into a view of the world that is cooperative, compassionate, and egalitarian. It implies that the teacher creates imaginative challenges for the children (there are dozens of brilliant and specific ones in this book), speaks with the children about what they are doing, listens carefully to what the children say, and follows their lead in the development of projects. In this context the teacher is not just a facilitator or coach. On the contrary, the teacher is an active participant who brings exercises and ideas to the learning situation, engages in doing those exercises along with the children, challenges the children to think and speak about what they are doing, and brings the work to the point where it can be shared both in the classroom and in the community. This inspiring vision of the teacher as artist and visionary walks the delicate line between didactic and hands-off teaching. Rodari's examples of how this works provide tonic to the often useless debates between authoritarian and free educators. Rodari develops a communal, creative, third way in which teachers and students are engaged in imaginative work and play together.

Many of Rodari's ideas were developed in the schools of Reggio Emilia. In addition to working directly with young children, Rodari worked with teachers and whole school staffs. Over the years his ideas have become part of the everyday fabric of schooling there. Recently "The Hundred Languages of Childhood," an art exhibit sponsored by The Council for Early Childhood Professional Recognition, has been traveling throughout the United States. It includes children's work, photographs, information about the Reggio Emilia philosophy, theoretical background, and teaching methods. The exhibit, along with the reports of many American educators who have visited the schools in Reggio Emilia, has begun to bring Rodari's ideas into early childhood education in the United States.

Though Rodari's work has been primarily with young children, his ideas can be adapted for use with students of all ages. Many of the ideas would work wonderfully in creative writing classes in high school and college. For example, in talking about Pinocchio, Rodari suggests that children think about what it would be like to be made of wood. The analysis can become more specific and complex. What would you eat? What would sleep mean? Whom and what would you fear? What would the rain do to you? What would happen if you broke a finger or leg? How long would you live and what would death mean? The metaphor of a wooden person can be varied and extended, as Rodari suggests, to a person made of marble, straw, chocolate, plastic, smoke, or marzipan.

It's easy to see how this could be done in language arts classes for students of all ages as a prelude to writing stories or developing improvisations and plays. In physics class one could extend the exercise by asking what it would be like to be made of quanta or waves, to be composed solely of electricity or light. This is not so far-fetched. Einstein said that one of the thought experiments he conducted during the time he was developing the theory of relativity was to imagine himself traveling along with a light wave. Many other scientists and mathematicians enter the imaginative realm of the objects they think about. Imaginative play of the sort Rodari so beautifully describes in this book is part of creative activity at every level.

Translator's Note and Acknowledgments

The present translation is based on *Grammatica della fantasia: Introduzione all'arte di inventare storie* (Turin: Einaudi, 1973). I omitted two chapters from this text—"Utilità di Giosuè Carducci" and "Il falso indovinello"—because they are of interest only to Italian readers. Otherwise, I have tried to render a faithful translation of Rodari's text in his spirit, which means that I have at times adapted and played with his notions so that they can be more readily grasped and appreciated by an English-speaking audience. Due to the fact that Rodari sought to intervene in the pedagogical debates in Italy during the 1960s and 1970s, some of his remarks are closely tied to the debates about reform education in Italy. Nevertheless, his overall theory and method, influenced by American and European thinkers, are still highly relevant and applicable to present-day debates about education in English-speaking countries. Therefore, wherever possible, I have sought to provide clear links between his provocative interventions in the Italy of his time and the need to develop a stimulating grammar of the imagination in English-speaking countries in our own time.

Special thanks to my wife Carol Dines, who helped me immensely with the translation and who shares my great admiration for Rodari's works. I also want to express my gratitude to Trinita Buldrini and Annalisa Margheri, who have helped me grasp some subtleties of the Italian language and Rodari's remarkable use of this language. I am also grateful to Herb Kohl for steering me toward Teachers & Writers Collaborative. Last but not least, I am very appreciative of the editorial work of Chris Edgar, Paola Mignone, Ron Padgett, Wayne Padgett, and Jessica Sager, who have also added a great dose of enthusiasm to this project.

Gianni Rodari, Devil's Advocate as Patron Saint of Children

by Jack Zipes

IN ITALY, Gianni Rodari would need no introduction. A household name among educators and parents, not to mention children, he is already considered by many literary historians to be Italy's most important writer of children's literature in the twentieth century.

But during the 1950s, when Rodari began writing poems, stories, and limericks for children, the Catholic Church regarded him as the devil's advocate and sought to have his works banned. In fact, his books were excluded by most schools up until the 1960s, and they were given scant attention by the press. Nevertheless, Rodari was not dismayed by this neglect or by attempts to dismiss his innovations and experiments in children's literature. Gradually, his imaginative work led to national and international recognition and acclaim. To a certain extent, there is a fairy tale element in the story about his rise from devil's advocate to saint, and it is a tale worth telling.

§

Rodari was born on October 23, 1920, in the town of Omegna on Lake d'Orta in northern Italy. His father Guiseppe was a baker, and his mother Maddalena, who had worked in France at different jobs for some time, assisted him in the shop. Since both parents were consumed by the demanding chores of running a bakery, Rodari was brought up by a wet-nurse in the nearby town of Pettenasco, as was his brother Cesare, born a year later.

When Rodari began school in Omegna, he tended to be shy and studious, with a penchant for solitude. In 1929, he was shaken by the death of his father. Rodari had greatly admired him, a warm and humane person, while his relationship to his mother, strict, religious, and rigid, remained problematical throughout his life. Nevertheless, he always knew that she made a great effort to provide him with a solid education and the means for a better life than she had led.

It was in 1929, the same year his father died, that the world depression erupted. Rodari's mother sold the bakery shop and moved to Gavirate, a town near Milan. She received a small pension, barely enough to support the family. In the meantime, Rodari continued to do well at school and showed a great interest in music. He sang in the church choir and learned how to play the piano and other instruments. He had also started writing poetry. From 1931 to 1934 he attended the seminary of San Pietro Martire di Seveso near Milan, but he hated the militaristic atmosphere of the school and stayed there only to please his mother. In 1934 he transferred to the Istituto Magistrale Manzoni in Varese, and due to his good marks, he received a scholarship. While there he took violin lessons and thought of becoming a professional musician. At this time, however, the depression was still in full force, and Rodari had to think of a more practical way of earning a living. Moreover, Italy was fully under the control of the fascists. Since he despised authoritarianism, Rodari tried to make political sense out of the distressing developments in Europe and to develop his own personal philosophy of life. Though still in high school, he had begun reading Schopenhauer, Stirner, and Nietzsche, as well as Marx's *Communist Manifesto*, "The Eighteenth Brumaire," and *The Poverty of Philosophy*. This mixture of thinkers typifies Rodari's method of work: he was always drawn to innovative thinkers, no matter what their political persuasion was, and grounded his own original thinking in European romantic and dialectic thought. This tendency is apparent in *The Grammar of Fantasy*, in which he refers to experimental writers like Novalis and André Breton, but also to pragmatic thinkers like John Dewey and Bertrand Russell. The bond that linked all these intellectuals who influenced him was their radicalism, that is, their desire to get at the root of things and push truth to its limits. Most important for Rodari was their reliance on autonomous and imaginative thinking.

But, at seventeen, Rodari himself had not yet formulated his own political philosophy. He received his *diploma maestro* in 1937, which meant he could teach in elementary schools. In 1938 he tutored the children of a German-Jewish refugee family for six months while learning German. Later in the year, he formed a group called Young Communists with some friends, but this tiny sect did not stay together very long. Rodari was still searching for a professional commitment and a way to bring together his interests in philosophy, teaching, and politics.

In 1939 he enrolled at the Catholic University of Milan, but after taking a few courses and passing examinations required for teachers, he abandoned his studies because the university was stifling his creativity. During the next two years he taught at schools in small cities of northern Italy. When Italy entered World War II in 1940, Rodari was fortunate not to be drafted, because of bad health. The following year he received an advanced teaching degree by passing a state examination, the *concorso da maestro*, and started teaching in the town of Uboldo. Unfortunately, unemployment in Italy and the financial predicament of his family forced Rodari to join the fascist party, a necessity if one wanted to be employed as a teacher at that time. Given such conditions, he was very pessimistic about the situation in Europe and his own future. In addition, two of his best friends died early in the war, and his brother was interned in a concentration camp in Germany in 1943. After the fall of the Italian fascist government in July 1943, Rodari saw more clearly that he had to take more of a political stand for his anti-fascist beliefs, and he helped form a communist cell group in Gavirate. In December he began working in a hospital in Milan, and the following year he joined the Resistance and became a member of the Communist Party.

At the close of World War II, Rodari, still only twenty-five, made up his mind to give up teaching and devote himself fully to the political programs of the Communist Party. To a certain extent, he never really abandoned teaching, for his writing always contained a strong didactic element, and eventually he re-entered schools through the back door during the 1970s. But at the end of the war, Rodari was totally committed to Marxist philosophy, especially to its utopian aspects, and he was intent on changing the world that had brought about so much oppression and injustice. Never again did he want to experience war or fascism.

In 1945 he went to the city of Varese to start a journal called *L'ordine nuovo* for the Communist Party, and it was there that he discovered his talent as a journalist, his career for life. By 1947 he was transferred to Milan to write for the communist newspaper *L'Unità*, and at one point was asked to compose some poems and stories for children. That is, it was by chance, as Rodari always liked to put it, that he began a "second" career, as a writer for children. Eventually, it would eclipse his journalism and enable him to express his social and political concerns in ways that he had never imagined.

It was due to his children's stories and his background as a teacher that, in 1950, the Communist Party sent Rodari to Rome to co-edit a weekly magazine for children called *Il pioniere*. In the early 1950s, the Communist Party was the largest in Italy, and its youth organization, the Association of Pioneers in Italy, had between 170,000 and 180,000 members. Thus Rodari had a large audience—albeit mostly people with socialist inclinations and children from the working classes—but it was exactly the audience that he desired, for he was committed to improving the situation of the young in a country that had been devastated by the war. After all, he was a baker's son who had risen from modest circumstances, and he felt in touch with the immense problems of Italian children. In turn, when children and educators read his work, they realized that Rodari was extraordinary, that his fantastical writing struck a chord of truth that had great meaning for their lives.

During the 1950s Rodari wrote hundreds of poems, stories, and songs for children that he published in different newspapers and magazines. His first two books, *Il libro delle filastrocche* (*The Book of Rhymes*, 1950) and *Il treno delle filastrocche* (*The Train of Rhymes*, 1952), were highly unusual anthologies of short poems that depicted the everyday life and experience of the masses and the working world for children, while pointing to the hypocrisy of Italian politics and politicians. Though the poems were similar to the limericks of Edward Lear and the nonsense verse of Lewis Carroll, they depicted the problems facing the poor in post-war Italy: unemployment, corruption, and authoritarian bureaucracy that still bore the mark of fascism. In addition to this poetry, he published two longer narratives that had a minimal success at that time, *Il romanzo di Cipollino* (*The Romance of Cipollino*, 1951), a fantastical novel that ridiculed the tyrannical behavior of a prince named Limone, and *Piccoli vagabondi* (*Small Vagabonds*, 1952), a realistic novel about two impoverished brothers, eight and nine years old, who are forced to wander about Italy after World War II, seeking work and refuge.

Rodari himself became more settled in Rome in the early 1950s, and in 1952 he invited his mother to come live with him. The following year he married Maria Teresa Ferretti, whom he had first met in 1948 in Modena, where she had been working as a secretary. In 1957, she gave birth to a daughter, Paola. It was in 1957 as well that Rodari was able to rent a larger apartment at the Villa Pamphili, where he lived until his death. During the 1950s Rodari's financial situation was always precarious because his books for children did not sell well, nor was his salary as a journalist very high. In fact, after *Il pioniere* ceased publication in 1953, Rodari worked for several magazines and newspapers that did not fare well. For instance, he directed *Avanguardia*, the new weekly of the Communist Youth Federation, from 1953 to 1956. But his interest in political journalism was waning, especially with the revelations about Stalinism in 1953. From 1956 to 1958 he worked briefly for *L'Unità* once more, and then in 1958 he joined *Paese sera*, an independent newspaper on the left but not aligned with any party. At the same time, he continued publishing highly unusual books for children, such as *La gondola fantasma* (*The Phantom Gondola*, 1955) and *Gelsomino nel paese dei bugiardi* (*Gelsomino in the*

Country of Liars, 1958). Yet, since most of his works were distributed by small publishing houses affiliated with the Communist Party or other socialist organizations, Rodari was not well known outside of leftist circles. Furthermore, the Church continually tried to brand him as a writer whose politics would corrupt the minds of children.

In 1960, two events enabled Rodari to reach a wider audience in Italy and to work more closely with children from all social classes. First, Einaudi, a major publisher, issued his *Filastrocche in cielo e in terra (Nonsense Rhymes in the Sky and on Earth)*. This was the first time that a publisher not associated with the Communist Party or other left-wing groups had promoted his work. The second event was more ironic. Due to various translations of Rodari's works in the Soviet Union, especially *Cipollino*, he had become somewhat famous there, and when this fame was reported by Italian newspapers in 1960, it stimulated interest in his works. Once Einaudi became Rodari's primary publisher and he gained the respect and recognition of the media, Rodari, the "devil's advocate," became more "appropriate" as a writer for children in the eyes of the general public and was invited into schools where he could test his stories with children and collaborate with teachers. Throughout the 1960s he worked with the Educational Cooperation Movement, and his experience in schools undoubtedly enabled him to experiment with his unique creative methods for stimulating children's imaginations. As a result of the stimulus he received from the new exchange with children and educators, several of his most significant works appeared during the 1960s: *Favole al telefono (Telephone Tales*, 1962); *Il pianeta degli alberi di Natale (The Planet of Christmas Trees*, 1962); *Atalanta, una fanciulla nella Grecia degli eroi e degli dei (Atalanta, A Young Girl of Ancient Greece*, 1963); *Il libro degli errori (The Book of Errors*, 1964); and *La torta in cielo (The Pie in the Sky*, 1966).

Strongly influenced by the avant-garde movements of the 1920s such as dadaism and futurism, Rodari was sort of a forerunner of magic realism, but one with a political commitment. All of his stories in *Favole al telefono* and *Il libro degli errori* are grounded in some kind of real incident that is quickly turned into an absurd if not nonsensical situation. However, it is through the most imaginative turn of events possible, Rodari suggests, that children can learn the truth about reality. The framework for the stories in *Favole al telefono*, for instance, is indicative of his technique. A traveling salesman misses his children so much that he calls them each night to tell them a story. The stories must be short, otherwise his telephone bills would be exorbitant. Thus, each tale is about two pages in length and concerns imaginary characters whom the father supposedly encounters during his trips. So unusual are the stories that the telephone operators and others (thanks to a vast party line) begin listening in on the tales that often deal with the strange customs and events in other lands. The effect is to encourage children to reflect upon their own customs.

From 1966 to 1969, Rodari was active in the reform movement in schools and gave numerous talks. He was particularly disturbed by the massive changes that were occurring in Italy. This was the period of great political unrest and modernization, and Rodari, who always paid close attention to the protests and the needs of the young, sought to record the pulse of his times, both in his fiction and in his pedagogical work. Once again, Rodari, still writing for various newspapers, entered a highly productive phase. After the publication of three collections of remarkable tales, *Venti storie più una* (*Twenty Stories Plus One*, 1969), *Tante storie per giocare* (*Many Stories for Play*, 1971), and *Novelle fatte a macchina* (*Stories Written by a Machine*), Rodari brought out his significant study, *Grammatica della fantasia*, in 1973. Not only did the ideas and methods in this book bear the fruit of approximately fifteen years of writing for children and working in schools, but they also emanated from stimulating exchanges that he had with teachers during a series of meetings held in the city of Reggio Emilia in March, 1972. Little did he know at that time that this small book would have an enormous impact on future generations of teachers and would serve, along with his fiction, as the basis for numerous projects in schools throughout Italy.

After the publication of *Grammatica della fantasia*, Rodari continued publishing such important works as *Marionette in libertà* (*Marionettes at Liberty*, 1974), *C'era due volte il barone Lamberto* (*Twice Upon a Time There Was Baron Lamberto*, 1978), *La gondola fantasma* (*The Phantom Gondola*, 1978), and *Il gioco dei quattro cantoni* (*The Game of Four Corners*, 1980). At the same time, he wrote for newspapers, made trips to Eastern Europe and the Soviet Union, and worked in schools.

By 1977, Rodari had become exhausted. He was no longer interested in writing for *Paese sera* or other newspapers. A physical checkup revealed that he had a blood clot in his leg that could prove fatal, and he took a leave from his newspaper. Unable to work, Rodari became depressed. Though he developed many projects and wrote about his visits and work with educators in the Soviet Union, he was not able to accomplish anything new. His health deteriorated, and eventually he was compelled to undergo an operation to improve his circulation. On April 11, 1980, he seemed to be recovering from the operation, which had lasted seven hours due to complications. But three days later he suddenly died of a heart attack.

Rodari's unexpected death was a great shock to his friends and to the Italian public. Though he had been suffering a great deal and had become irritable, he was still conceiving plans for the future that he hoped would help to enlighten and entertain children at the same time. This hope was not eclipsed by his death, for hundreds if not thousands of writers and educators have continued his work in Italy, while Einaudi and Editori Riuniti, Rodari's two major publishers, have produced numerous important posthumous works and have made available all his key works written between 1950 and 1980.

It is difficult to say which is more important, Rodari's literary or pedagogical work. The fact is, it is impossible to separate one from the other, just as it is to divide Rodari into separate categories. Rodari was a teacher, Communist, journalist, poet, musician, theoretician, and writer for children, all in one. Perhaps no work of his makes his multi-faceted life more clear than *The Grammar of Fantasy*, but this work is not only significant for what it reveals about Rodari's thinking and talents. This book is a classic manual for educators interested in stimulating children to develop their own writing and reading skills in a manner that will enable children to gain greater autonomy. It is a classic that will never age, because Rodari grasped children's need to play with life's rules by using the grammar of their own imaginations. Moreover, he understood that children need the guidance of compassionate adults to help them decipher the contradictions in their lives. In fact, if there is one phrase that might best describe Rodari's project in *The Grammar of Fantasy*, it is compassion for children, combined with respect for educators and their ideas and experiments.

Rodari begins with the premise that children's lives are highly proscribed and that, if they are to learn to act and think for themselves, they must acquire playful methods and techniques that will enable them to fathom what the words, expressions, forms, and shapes of their culture mean. They must be encouraged to question, challenge, destroy, mock, eliminate, generate, and reproduce their own language and meanings through stories that will enable them to narrate their own lives. In the process, Rodari reflects upon how children learn and demonstrates that the imagination has rules of its own that must be respected if children are to respond and seek more knowledge about language and the imagination. In this respect, he anticipated the contemporary provocative linguistic studies that posit language as innate, that children instinctively know the structures of language long before they are taught them.

For Rodari, imagination is a force that enables children to put language into effect on their behalf, and, as such, the imagination has its own "grammar" that can be cultivated for either beneficial or detrimental ends. According to Rodari, seeing language and story as set and fixed by absolute rules is detrimental to the intellectual growth of children. What benefits children most, he believed, is empowerment in a communal context, not the individualism that is so common in the United States. In all his pedagogical and literary projects Rodari emphasized the social context of learning to share and be considerate of others. Just as he believed that two highly unlikely words could always be linked and become fruitful, he felt that different types of children could come together and use their imaginations together to grasp and solve their personal and social problems. Through a dialectical process of composition-decomposition-recomposition of words, Rodari demonstrated that children can confront essential personal and political problems in their everyday lives. For Rodari, the skills that children uncover in this process will enable them to invent stories that make life much more than a question of survival. Indeed, life can be rife with deep pleasure and political significance.

Rodari did not preach. Nor did he talk down to children and other educators. As a teacher he was always a learner at the same time. In *The Grammar of Fantasy*, one can almost hear Rodari testing each one of his words, waiting for a response, and trying to incorporate that response into his next provocative suggestion. He was, of course, a provocateur, but a gentle one with a great ironic wit. The child spoke through him, the playful child who could not contain his curiosity and who rejected arbitrary rules—including the arbitrary aspects of grammar, schools, governments, and institutions. This is why Rodari was so concerned with working with children and developing rules of respect and cooperation. He never stopped thinking of children. He never stopped inventing stories. He never stopped questioning the status quo. His *Grammar of Fantasy* reveals not only important practical methods for guiding the imagination of children, but also the amazing spirit of a man who refused to let his dreams of a better world die, and who has passed them on to us.

Preface

IN THE WINTER of 1937–38, I was recommended by a teacher, the wife of a policeman, to tutor the children of German Jews, who thought that they had found refuge in Italy from the racist persecutions in their homeland. Indeed, they thought this only for a few months. I lived with them in a farmhouse in the hills near Lake Maggiore, and I worked with the children from seven till ten in the morning. The rest of the day I spent walking in the woods and reading Dostoevsky. It was a wonderful time as long as it lasted. I learned a little German, and I threw myself into reading books written in German, with the passion, fury, and desire that are a hundred times more fruitful for young people than a hundred years of school.

One day, as I was reading the *Fragments* of Novalis (1772–1801), I found the following phrase: "If there were a theory of the fantastic like there is in the case of logic, then we would be able to discover the art of invention." It was wonderful. Almost all of Novalis' aphoristic "fragments" are like this. Almost all contain extraordinary revelations.

Some months later, after I had become acquainted with the work of the French surrealists, I thought I had found in their method of working that very theory of the fantastic that Novalis had sought. To be sure, André Breton, the father and prophet of surrealism, had written in the first manifesto of the movement: "The future surrealist techniques do not interest me." But his friends among the writers and painters were the very ones who had invented all kinds of methods that were to be useful in the future. At that time I was teaching in elementary schools because the Jewish family had left Italy in search of another homeland. I must have been a bad teacher, poorly prepared for my work. My head was stuffed with everything possible, from Indo-European linguistics to Marxism. (Even though Signor Romussi, a gentleman and director of the public library in Varese, had a picture of Mussolini in plain sight over his desk, he handed me every book that I requested, never blinking an eye.) Clearly, my head was stuffed with everything except those things that pertained directly to school. Perhaps it was because of this that I was not a boring teacher. I told the children stories, partly out of sympathy for them, partly out of a desire to play, stories without the least reference to reality or to good common sense. And most of these stories were ones that I invented by making use of the "techniques" that Breton had promoted and at the same time deprecated.

It was during this time that I ceremoniously gave a notebook the title *Notes on the Fantastic.* I did not actually record the stories that I had been telling. Rather, I took notes about the manner in which they had originated, the tricks that I had discovered, or believed that I had discovered, in order to set words and images in motion.

For a long time I had forgotten and buried all of this until, in 1948, I happened to start writing for children, almost by chance. Now the "fantastic" came back to me, and I developed it further, using it in my new and unexpected profession. Only my laziness and a certain reluctance concerning systems as well as a lack of time prevented me from talking about this in public until 1962, when I published "Guidelines for Inventing Stories" in two parts for the Roman daily, *Paese sera*, on February 9th and 19th.

In these articles I kept a respectful distance from the subject matter, pretending to have received it from a young Japanese scholar with whom I had become acquainted during the Olympics. He supposedly gave me a manuscript containing the English translation of a little work that had been published in Stuttgart during 1912 by the Novalis Verlag, which a certain Otto Schlegel-Kamnitzer had allegedly written under the title, *The Fundamentals of the Fantastic: The Art of Writing Fairy Tales*. Within the frame of this fictitious work, which was not very original, I laid out some simple techniques of invention, partly serious, partly in fun. They were the same that I was to use and impart for years in all the schools in which I told stories and responded to the children's questions. There is always one child who will ask a question, and it will be exactly like this: "What do you have to do to invent a story?" This question deserves an honest answer.

I returned to this subject later in the *Giornale dei genitori* (*The Parents' Newspaper*) by offering suggestions to readers about how they themselves could tell "Good-Night Stories." ("What Happens when Grandfather Becomes a Cat?" December, 1969; "A Plate Full of Stories," January–February, 1971; "Stories for Laughing," April, 1971).

It seems horrible to write these dates in a chronological row. Who could really be interested in them? Nevertheless, I like writing them down, one after the other, as if they were important. The reader may bear in mind that I am playing the game that transactional psychology calls "Look, Mom! No hands!" It is always wonderful to be able to boast about something. . . .

§

In 1972, I was invited by the city administration of Reggio Emilia to conduct a series of meetings with approximately fifty teachers levels K–12 from March 6–10. On this occasion I presented and summarized all my professional techniques, so to speak, in an official and definitive manner.

Three things will make me remember this week as one of the most wonderful of my life. The first was the poster the municipal council had made for this occasion, announcing the conference with the words "Meetings with the Fantastic." Consequently, I could read on scattered walls of the city the word that had accompanied me for thirty-four years. The second was the notice on the poster that the "registration" was limited to "fifty participants." A larger number would have evidently transformed the meetings into lectures that would not have been useful for anyone. But the notice seemed to express the fear that, as a result of the call of the "fantastic," uncontrollable crowds of people might storm the meeting hall, a former training hall for firefighters, with iron pillars painted violet. It was very moving that they expected such a storm of people. The third and most substantial reason for my happiness was due to the fact that I was being given the opportunity to have long and detailed discussions about the function of the imagination and about techniques to stimulate it. There would be constant questions, demonstrations of my work, and conversations with the participants. In addition, I could discuss how the techniques might be disseminated so that everyone could use them, for example, as instruments for the linguistic education of children, but not just for this purpose alone.

At the end of this "brief course" I was able to obtain the texts of five conversations, thanks to tape recordings and the patience of a stenographer.

The present book is a revision of the discussions that I had in Reggio Emilia. It is not—and I want to make this clear here—an attempt to establish a "fantastics" with rules ready to be taught and studied in schools like geometry. Nor is it a complete theory of the imagination and invention, for which more muscle power and someone less ignorant than me would be necessary. Moreover, this book is not even an "essay." In fact, I really do not know what it is. It talks about some ways of inventing stories for children and helping children to invent their own stories. But who knows how many other ways could be found and described? Here I deal only with invention via words and try to suggest, without going too deeply into the matter, that the techniques can easily be transformed into other modes of expression and be used when a story is told by a single teller or by a group. In addition, they can serve as the basis of theater or the script for a puppet play. They can be developed to produce comics and films or cassettes taped and sent to friends. In fact, these techniques can be incorporated into all kinds of children's games, but I do not say much about this point.

I hope that this small book can be useful for all those people who believe it is necessary for the imagination to have a place in education; for all those who trust in the creativity of children; and for all those who know the liberating value of the word. "Every possible use of words should be made available to every single person"—this seems to me to be a good motto with a democratic sound. Not because everyone should be an artist but because no one should be a slave.

1 • The Stone in the Pond

A STONE THROWN into a pond sets in motion concentric waves that spread out on the surface of the water, and their reverberation has an effect on the water lilies and reeds, the paper boat and the buoys of the fishermen at various distances. All these objects are just there for themselves, enjoying their tranquility, when they are wakened to life, as it were, and are compelled to react and to enter into contact with one another. Other invisible vibrations spread into the depths, in all directions, as the stone falls and brushes the algae, scaring the fish and continually causing new molecular movements. When it then touches the bottom, it stirs up the mud and bumps into things that have rested there forgotten, some of which are dislodged, others buried once again in the sand. In a short time countless events or micro-events occur one after another. Even if a person had the time and desire, I doubt whether all of this could be registered without missing some aspect of change.

It is not much different with a word, thrown by chance into the mind, producing waves on the surface and in the depths. It provokes an infinite series of chain reactions and, as it falls, it evokes sounds and images, analogues and recollections, meanings and dreams, in a movement that touches experience and memory, the imagination and the unconscious, and is complicated by the fact that the mind itself does not react passively, but intervenes continually to accept and reject these representations, to connect and censor them, construct and destroy them.

Take the word *stone* as an example. When it falls into the mind, it drags words after it, bumps into words, or avoids them. In short, it comes into contact with them in different ways:

• with all the words that begin with *s* but do not continue with *t*, like "seminar," "silence," "system"

• with all the words that begin with *st*, like "stamp," "stem," "start," "stag," "stop," "stink"

• with all the words that rhyme with it, like "bone," "tone," "phone," "cone," "drone"

• with all the words that come close in meaning according to the dictionary, like "rock," "pebble," "marble," "brick," "granite"

• et cetera.

These are the easiest associations. A word collides with another one through gravity. This is hardly sufficient to ignite sparks (but one can never know).

Meanwhile the word falls in other directions, sinks into a past world, and lets sunken existences emerge. At first contact, *stone* is for me Santa Caterina del Sasso, a sanctuary situated on a steep rocky cliff over Lake Maggiore. I rode there on my bike, and I also went there with my friend Amedeo. We would sit down beneath a cool portico to drink white wine and to talk about Kant. Because we commuted to school together, we also met each other on the train. Amedeo wore a long blue coat. On some days one could detect the outlines of his violin case beneath it. Since the handle of my case was broken, I had to carry it under my arm. Amedeo joined the mountain troops during the war and was killed in Russia.

Another time Amedeo's figure returned to me as I was "digging" for the word *brick*, which reminded me of certain low baking ovens in the countryside of Lombardy, of long walks in the fog or in the woods. Amedeo and I frequently spent entire afternoons in the woods talking about Kant and Dostoevsky and the poets Eugenio Montale and Alfonso Gatto. The friendships at sixteen are those that leave the most profound marks on our lives. But that is not what concerns me here. I am concerned with perceiving how any word chosen by chance can function as a magical word to exhume fields of memory that have rested under the dust of time.

The taste of the madeleine had the same effect in Proust's memory. And after him all the "writers of times past" have learned, even too much, to listen to the buried echoes of words, their smells, and their sounds. But we want to invent stories for children, not write tales to recuperate and preserve our "things past." From time to time it is entertaining and useful to play the memory game, even with children. Any word can help them remember "that time when . . . ," to discover themselves in the time that is passing, to measure the distance between today and yesterday, even if their "yesterdays" are fortunately still small in number and not so packed with events.

The theme of the fantastic stems from this kind of search that takes off from one single word. Whenever unusual unions are created, whenever there are complex movements of images and capricious overlappings, an unpredictable affinity is illuminated between words that belong to different chains. *Brick* brings with it: sick, tick, lick, stick, click, nick, kick. . . .

Brick and *stick* seem to me to be an interesting pair, even if not so "beautiful as the chance encounter of an umbrella and a sewing machine on an operating table" (Lautréamont, *Les chants de Maldoror*). In the confusing play of words that have been evoked, *brick* coincides with *stick* like *stone* with *bone.* Amedeo's violin probably introduces an emotional element and influences the emergence of a musical image:

> Here we have the house full of music. It is made out of musical bricks, musical stones. Its walls, due to the percussion of small hammers, produce all possible tones. I know that there is a C sharp over the couch. The clearest F sharp is under the window. The floor is entirely in B flat major, an exciting tone. There is an amazing atonal, serial electronic door. It is enough just to touch them with one's finger to produce an entire piece in the manner of Nono-Berio-Maderna. Stockhausen would become delirious about this. (He fits perfectly into this picture more than any other musician, since the word "Haus," house, is incorporated in his name.) But I am not solely concerned with a house. There is an entire musical country with a piano house, a bell house, a bassoon house. It is an orchestra village. In the evening the inhabitants organize a beautiful concert from their houses before they go to bed. . . . At night, when they are all asleep, a prisoner plays on the bars of his cell. . . . Et cetera. Now the story has begun.

I think that the prisoner entered the story because of the rhyme *bell* and *cell.* I was not consciously aware of the rhyme, but apparently it was lurking in the background. One could say that the prison bars simply manifested themselves. But I don't believe it. Rather my memory must have quickly brought it to the surface and suggested it to me from the title of an old film: *Prison without Bars.*

The imagination can now follow another path:

> All the bars of all the prisons in the world are taken down. Everyone will become free. Even the thieves? Yes, even the thieves. It is prison that produces thieves. Put an end to the prisons, put an end to thieves. . . .

At this point I can note how my ideology makes its mark in an ostensibly mechanical process, like the block of a stamp, but it also modifies the stamp itself. I hear the echo of past and recent readings. The world of the excluded asks arrogantly to be named: orphanages, reform schools, homes for the aged, insane asylums, schoolrooms. Reality erupts into the surrealistic exercise. In the end, if the musical country becomes a story, it will not be treated in an evasive fantastical manner, but in a way that will rediscover and represent reality in new forms.

But the exploration of the word *stone* is not finished. I must negate it as an organism that has a certain meaning and a certain sound and break it down into its letters disclosing words that I set down one after another to arrive at its pronunciation.

I write the letters beneath each other:

S -
T -
O -
N -
E -

Now I can write next to each letter the first word that comes to my mind, and in this way I obtain a new series. (For example: sand-top-oven-news-earthquake.) Or I can—this is more entertaining—write five words next to each letter that produce a logical sentence. For example:

S - Seven
T - tigers
O - oppose
N - nasty
E - enemies.

At this moment I do not know what to do with the seven tigers except to make a nonsense rhyme out of them:

Seven tigers snub their nose
Even when they smell a rose . . . et cetera.

But one should not expect a significant result on first try. I'll try another series with the same system:

S - Seventeen
T - tyrants
O - oppress
N - noble
E - elephants.

Seventeen is an automatic extension of the previous *seven*. The tyrants are evidently an intensification of the powerful tigers. Instead of opposing enemies, these tyrants exploit noble elephants, and we are left with a dramatic image.

I myself have invented many stories simply by choosing a word by chance. One time, for example, I took off from the word *omnibus* and made the following playful association: omnibus-Columbus. (Please excuse this arbitrary use of a famous name, which is not entirely arbitrary, and for introducing it into an area that also touches on fairy tales.) The omnibus of Columbus—only a bus—the wheels of a bus—the round *o*—round earth—round egg—oval—orbit. All these associations led me to write a story entitled "A World in an Egg" that was a combination of non-sense and science fiction.

Now we can let the word *stone* find its destiny. But we should not delude ourselves and think that we have exhausted its possibilities. Paul Valéry once said, "There is not a single word that can be grasped even when we get to the bottom of it." And Wittgenstein stated: "Words are like a thin surface over deep water." This is why stories are found when we dive for them.

In connection with the word *brick*, I recall an American creativity test that Marta Fattori discusses in her book *Creatività ed educazione* (*Creativity and Education*). The children who took this test were asked to count all the possible uses of bricks that they knew or could imagine. Perhaps this is why the word *brick* imposed itself on me with such insistence, for I had only recently come upon this test in Fattori's book. Unfortunately, tests of this kind are not intended to stimulate the creativity of children. Rather, they are mainly used to measure and select the "most imaginative" children, like other tests that select the "smartest in math." Of course, they may have their use. But in essence they follow goals that are well above the heads of the children.

On the other hand, the game of "the stone in the pond," which I have briefly illustrated here, moves in the opposite direction: it tends to be useful for children rather than to use them.

2 · The Word *Hi*

SOME YEARS AGO The Storyteller Game was developed in the elementary schools of the city of Reggio Emilia. The children climbed onto an easy chair, as though it were a stage, and took turns telling their playmates, who squatted on the floor, stories that they invented by themselves. The teacher transcribed the stories, and all the children paid close attention to make sure that she did not forget or change anything. Then the children would illustrate their stories with large drawings. I shall analyze one of these spontaneous stories later in this chapter, but right now I want to use The Storyteller Game to preface my comments.

After I had spoken about the way stories can be invented by building on a given word, Giulia Notari, a teacher at Diana primary school in Reggio Emilia, asked her pupils whether any of them felt like inventing a story with the new system and suggested the word *hi*. Then a boy of five told the following story:

A boy had lost all the good words, and only the bad ones remained: shit, turd, shithead, et cetera.

So his mother takes him to a doctor with a long moustache, and he says, "Open your mouth, stick your tongue out, look up, look down, take a deep breath, and blow."

Then the doctor tells him to go and look around for a good word. The first word he finds is like this [he demonstrates with his fingers a tiny word about an inch in length], and it is a bad word—*damn*. Then he finds a long word like this (he demonstrates another word about three inches in length), and it is *shitty*, a bad word. Then he finds a little pink word which is *hi*. He puts it in his pocket, takes it home, and learns to speak the word in a nice way and becomes good.

While the boy told the story, the other children intervened two times to pick up key words and develop them in the story. The first time they gleefully improvised "bad" words with a litany of bad language, and they added all the bad words that they knew and made up new ones evoked by the first "term" they heard in the story. They did it openly and provocatively in a liberating game of excremental comedy that is familiar to anyone who has had something to do with children. From a technical viewpoint, the game of associations developed from what linguists call the "axis of selection" (Roman Jakobson), like a search for related words along a chain of meanings. However, these words did not represent a diversion, an abandonment of the theme of the story. On the contrary, they clarified and helped determine the plot. In the work of a poet, Jakobson states, the "axis of selection" projects itself onto the "axis of combination." A sound (a rhyme) can evoke a meaning; a verbal analogy can produce a metaphor. When a child invents a story, the same thing occurs. We are dealing here with a creative process that also has an aesthetic aspect, but what interests us here is its relationship to creativity, not to art.

The second time that the listeners interrupted the storyteller was to develop the "doctor game" and to find variations for the customary "stick out your tongue." Here the amusement had a second meaning, a psychological one—it served to defuse the dramatic appearance of the doctor figure, who is always somewhat feared, by making fun of him. In addition, there was the contest about who could find the most surprising and most original variations ("look up, look down"). A game of this genre is already theater, and it is the most basic step in dramatization.

But let us turn to the structure of the story. In reality it is not based exclusively on the word *hi*, that is, on its meaning and its sound. The boy who began the story took the entire expression "the word *hi*" as motif. This is why the search for related and similar words did not predominate in his imagination—although this did occur at another point in time—nor did the search for situations in which the word is used in this or that way. Even its most simple use as greeting seems essentially to have been rejected. Instead, the expression "the word *hi*" gave rise directly on its "axis of selection" to the construction of two categories of words: the "good words" and the "bad words" and ultimately, through the gestures, to two other categories, the "short" and the "long" words.

The boy's gesture was not improvised but rather appropriated. He had certainly seen the popular Italian TV commercial for a certain kind of candy in which two hands clap, and at the end, the name of the candy is displayed between the two hands. The boy had fished up this gesture from his memory and made use of it in an original and personal way. He had rejected the message of the commercial and had picked up its implicit and non-intended and non-programmed message—the gesture that measures the length of words. One can never be certain what a child learns while watching TV. And one should never underestimate his or her capacity to react creatively.

In the story, the censorship exercised by the cultural standard intervenes just at the right moment. The boy defines those words as "bad" that he has been taught to consider inappropriate. But the boy is in an educational environment that can overcome certain conditioning. Diana is a non-repressive school in which the children are not reprimanded or scolded when they use bad words. From this perspective, the most extraordinary result of this story consists in the ultimate abandonment of those classes of words that were introduced at the beginning.

The "bad" words that the boy encounters in his search—*damn, shitty*—are not "bad" in relation to the standard of repression. Rather, they are words that drive people away, that offend others, that do not enable one to make friends, to be together and play together. They are not the opposite of the abstract "good" words, but the opposite of the "right and friendly" words. Here a new category of words is born, showing new values that the boy has absorbed at school. The child's mind arrived at this result by reacting to his own images, judging them and governing their associations with the contribution of his entire small personality in action. And it is clear why *hi* must be a "little pink word." Pink is a friendly, delicate, and non-aggressive color. The color is an indication of value. Nevertheless, it is a shame that the boy was not asked: "Why pink?" His answer would have told us something that we did not know and is now extremely difficult to reconstruct.

3 • The Fantastic Binominal

WE HAVE SEEN the motif of the fantastic—the beginning for a story—originate from a single word. But we are dealing here with an optical illusion more than anything else. In reality one electrical pole is not enough to cause a spark; it takes two. The single word "acts" only when it encounters a second that provokes it and compels it to leave the track of habit and to discover new possibilities of meaning. To live means to struggle.

This is due to the fact that the imagination is not just a faculty separate from the mind. It is the mind itself in its entirety, which, applied to one activity more than another, always makes use of the same procedures. And the mind is born out of struggle, not out of tranquility. Henri Wallon wrote in his book *Les Origines de la pensée chez l'enfant* (*The Origins of Thinking in the Child*) that thought is formed in pairs. The idea of soft cannot be formed before or after the idea of hard, but simultaneously in an encounter that is the offspring: "The fundamental element of thought is this binary structure, not the single elements that compose it. The couple, the pair precedes the isolated element."

Hence, in the beginning was this opposition. And Paul Klee was also of this opinion when he stated in his *Writings about Form and the Theory of Figures* that "a concept is impossible without its opposite. Concepts do not exist alone for themselves; rather they are, as a rule, 'conceptual binominals.'"

A story can be born only out of a "fantastic binominal."

"Horse-dog" is not really a "fantastic binominal." It is a simple association within the same zoological classification. At the evocation of the two four-legged animals, the imagination remains indifferent. It is a major third chord that does not promise anything exciting.

It is necessary to have a certain distance between the two words. One must be sufficiently strange or different from the other, and their coupling must be discreetly unusual, because the imagination is compelled to set itself in motion to establish a relationship between the two and to construct a (fantastic) whole in which the two foreign elements can live together. Therefore, it is best to choose the fantastic binominal with the help of chance. The two words should be dictated by two children without each other's knowledge, chosen at random, and indicated by blindly pointing at two pages of a dictionary that are far apart from one another.

When I was a teacher, I had one child go to the movable blackboard to write a word on one side, and another child to write a word on the reverse side. A certain expectation was created through this little preparatory ritual. If a child wrote the word *dog* in front of everyone, this word was already a special word, triggered to contribute to a surprise, to insert itself into an unpredictable event. This dog was not just any kind of a four-legged animal. It was already an adventurous, disposable, and fantastic character. When the blackboard was turned around, one could read, let us say, the word *closet*. It was greeted by a burst of laughter. The word *platypus* or *tetrahedron* would not have had a greater success. Now, a closet by itself would normally not cause anyone to laugh or cry. It is an inert object, a banality. But this closet, coupled with a dog, was something completely different. It was a discovery, an invention, an exciting stimulus.

Some years later I read what Max Ernst had written to explain his concept of the "systematic shift of space." He really made use of the image of the closet that de Chirico had portrayed in a classical landscape between olive trees and Greek temples. By "shifting the space" this way, thrown into an unrelated context, the closet became a mysterious object. Perhaps it was full of clothes, perhaps not. But it was certainly full of fascination.

Victor Shklovsky describes the "estrangement effect" that Tolstoy achieves when he talks about a simple couch in words that one would use when talking to a person who had never seen a couch before and would not have the slightest idea of how a couch could be used.

In the "fantastic binominal," the words are not taken in their daily meaning, but freed from the verbal chains that hold them together on a daily basis. They are "estranged," "shifted," thrown against one another in a sky that has never been seen before. Hence they are in the best possible condition for generating a story.

At this point let us take the words *dog* and *closet* once more. The most simple method for creating a connection between the two is by coupling them with prepositions. In this way we obtain different pictures:

1) the dog with the closet
2) the closet of the dog
3) the dog in the closet
4) the dog on the closet
5) et cetera.

Each one of these pictures offers us the outline of a fantastic situation:

1) A dog runs down the street *with a closet on his back*. It is his little basket. What can one do about it? The dog always carries it with him just like a snail carries its house. Continue this as you wish.

2) *The closet of the dog* seems to me more than anything else to be an idea for architects, designers, and interior decorators of luxurious apartments. The closet is there to hang up the dog's little coat, his different

muzzles and leashes, his overshoes for chilly days, back warmer with tassels, rubber bones, cat traps, a map of the city (in order to know where to go to fetch the milk, newspaper, and cigarettes for his master). The closet may also contain a story, but I don't have the faintest clue whether it does or doesn't.

3) *The dog in the closet* is much more inviting to hear and believe. Doctor Polyfemo comes home, opens the closet to take out his house jacket, and finds a dog inside. Right away, we are challenged to think up an explanation, to explain this apparition. But the explanation can wait. For the moment it is more interesting to analyze the situation at hand. The dog's breed cannot be ascertained. Perhaps it is a dog that sniffs out truffles. Perhaps it is a dog that sniffs cyclamens or rhododendrons. He is friendly, wags his tail, holds up his paw politely, but he refuses to get out of the closet, no matter how hard Dr. Polyfemo implores him. So Dr. Polyfemo decides to take a shower and finds a second dog, in the bathroom medicine cabinet. There is another one on the kitchen shelves, one in the dishwasher, another half frozen in the freezer. A poodle is in the pantry with the brooms, a Pekinese in the drawer of his desk. At this point Dr. Polyfemo could call the super to help him drive out the invaders, but the super happens to be a dog lover. So instead he runs to the butcher to buy twenty pounds of meat for his guests. And he does so for many days. But these acts draw attention. The butcher becomes suspicious. People begin to talk. Nasty rumors spread. Disparaging remarks. Is Dr. Polyfemo hiding atomic spies in his house? Is he possibly conducting diabolic experiments with all those pieces and slices of meat? The poor doctor loses his clientele. The police receive tips. The police chief orders the doctor's house to be searched. And in this way the people discover that Dr. Polyfemo had innocently suffered all this persecution out of love for the dogs. Et cetera.

At this stage the story is only "raw material." It would be the task of a writer to work it into a finished product. But the only thing that interests me here is to exemplify the use of the "fantastic binominal." The nonsense can remain the way it is. What concerns me is a technique that children know extremely well how to apply with the greatest pleasure, as I myself have seen in many Italian schools. Of course, the exercise has its real meaning, and I shall talk about this in later chapters. Yet one should not overlook how much joy it brings. In our schools there is too little laughter, if I may generalize. The idea that the education of a mind must be a dismal affair is among the most difficult things to overcome. Giacomo Leopardi had a great deal to say about this when he wrote in his *Zibaldone* ("Miscellaneous Notes") on August 1, 1823:

The most beautiful and happiest period of human beings, childhood, is plagued in a thousand ways with a thousand anxieties, troubles, and hardships of education and instruction to such an extent that the grown adult, even in the midst of all unhappiness, would refuse to become a child again if it meant suffering the same things that he or she had suffered in childhood.

4 • "Light" and "Shoes"

THE FOLLOWING STORY was invented by a boy, five and a half years old, with the participation of three of his friends, at Diana primary school in Reggio Emilia. The fantastic binominal that generated this story—"light" and "shoes"—was suggested by the teacher (the day after we had discussed this technique in our course). Without further ado, here it is:

> There was once a boy who was always putting on his father's shoes. One evening his father became sick and tired of his son always taking his shoes. So he hung him on the lamp, and then at midnight the boy fell down, and so the father said, "Who's there? A burglar?"
>
> He went to look and found his son on the ground all lit up. So the father tried to twist his son's head, but he did not go out. He tried to pull his earlobes, but he did not go out. He tried to push his nose, but he did not go out. He tried to press his bellybutton, but he did not go out. He tried to take off the shoes and succeeded. The boy was turned off.

This final idea—which had not been suggested by the principal narrator but by one of his three friends—pleased the other children so much that they burst into applause. In fact, this image was the perfect and logical end to the story and rounded out the narrative. But perhaps it did much more.

I believe that Doctor Freud himself would have been deeply moved, even his ghost, if he had heard this story that could easily be interpreted in terms of the Oedipus Complex. Or even if he had heard just the beginning of the story, with the boy who puts on his father's shoes and who wants to be, in effect, in his father's shoes as head of the family and to take his place next to the mother. An unequal struggle strewn with images of death. "To hang something" also means "to attach," "to hang on." And the boy was "on the ground" or "in the ground"? There should be no doubt about the ending if one correctly reads it—"he succeeds in turning him off" (i.e., extinguishing him)—which gives the drama a tragic conclusion. "To extinguish" (*spegnersi*) and "to die" (*morire*) are synonyms in Italian: "He has been extinguished by the kiss of the Lord" is an Italian expression that can be found in the obituaries posted on walls. Here the older and stronger man triumphs. He triumphs at midnight, the witching hour. And before the death there is torture such as the "twisting of the head," the "pulling of the ears," the "pushing of the nose."

I shall not insist in this exercise on this unauthorized psychoanalytic interpretation. Let the specialists have their say here: "videant consules" ("Senators, be careful").

If the unconscious appropriates the fantastic binominal in order to stage its dramas, it seems to me that the exact point of its intervention is the immediate echo produced by the word *shoe* in the experience of children. All children play at putting on the shoes of their fathers and mothers. To be "them." To be older. But also, more simply, to be "somebody else." Aside from its symbolical importance, the game of make-believe and dress-up is always pleasurable because of the grotesque effects that result from it. It is theater: to disguise oneself in the clothes of someone else, to play a role, to invent a life, to discover new gestures. It is a shame that, as a rule, children are permitted to disguise themselves only at Halloween or Mardi Gras, to put on masks, to wear their fathers' jackets or their grandmothers' undergarments. There should always be a hamper in the house filled with discarded clothes that can be used for make-believe games. At the primary school in Reggio Emilia there is not only a hamper for this purpose but an entire wardrobe. In Rome, all sorts of suits and evening clothes, no longer in fashion, are sold at the market of Via Sannio. When our daughter was little, we used to go there to fill the hamper that we had at home. All her friends liked our house just because of this hamper.

Why does the boy remain "all lit up"? Perhaps the most plausible reason for this can be found in the analogy: "hung" on the lamp, like a light bulb, the boy behaves like a light bulb. This explanation would be sufficient if the boy had turned himself on like a light the moment his father had "hung" him. But at this precise point in the story there is no mention of turning him on as a light. We see the boy "lit up" only after he has fallen to the ground. I believe that the imagination needs a few moments to discover this analogy, because the analogy does not reveal itself directly via the "visual"—the narrator "sees" the boy "hung," he sees him "turned on"— but becomes apparent through the axis of the verbal selection. In the consciousness of the boy there has been work on the side—while the story continued—and this work was filled with the echoes of the word *hung*. So we have the chain: "hung" (*appeso*), "attached" (*attaccato*), and "turned on" (*acceso*). The verbal analogy and the implied rhyme (in Italian) also make the analogy of the visual image apparent. In sum, it has been that work of "condensation of images" that Doctor Freud—always him, that blessed

Viennese doctor—described so well when he studied the creative processes of the dream. In this regard the story appears to be like a "dream with open eyes." It has all the atmosphere of a dream, the tendency toward the absurd, the motifs pressed together.

One leaves this atmosphere with the attempts of the father to "extinguish" the "boy-light-bulb." The variations on this theme are generated by the analogy, but they move on different levels: the experiences of the necessary movements of turning out a light (unscrewing a light bulb, pushing a button, pulling out an electrical cord, et cetera) are brought into play as well as the experience of one's own body. (It is this way that one moves from the head, to the ears, the nose, bellybutton, et cetera.) The game is at this point a collective one. The principal narrator has been only the detonator of an explosion in which everyone is involved—with an effect that the cyberneticists would call "amplification."

While searching for the variants, the children look at one another, search for the trace of a new idea on the bodies of their neighbors. The present intervenes in the story; its figures suggest new meanings in a process that in a certain way is similar to the workings of the rhyme. As the poet works, his or her process dictates meanings that are to a certain extent outside of the lyrical situation. The actions are also rhymed, even if not according to sound. They are "rhymed pairs," that is, they are most simple, just as those in a rhyme for children.

The variation at the end—"he takes off the shoes, and then he goes out"—represents an even more decisive break with the dream. It is a logical conclusion. There were the father's shoes, which had "turned on" the boy, for everything had begun with those shoes. It is sufficient to take off the shoes, and the light disappears. The story can come to an end. In essence, a logical idea conducted the magical instrument—"the father's shoes"—in the opposite direction of its initial movement.

In the moment the children make this discovery, they introduce the mathematical element of "reversibility" as metaphor into the free play of the imagination, but not yet as concept. They get to the concept much later. In the meantime, perhaps the fairy tale image has laid the groundwork for the elaboration of the concept.

One last remark (the last one only by pure chance, of course) concerns the insertion of "values" into the story. If one reads the story in this way, it is a tale about a disobedient boy who is punished within the framework of a cultural model that has been too traditional. The father is the one whom one must obey and who has the right to punish. Censorship has intervened to keep the story within the bounds of family morals.

After censorship's intervention, one can say that heaven and earth, as it were, have influenced the story: the unconscious (with its conflicts), experience, memory, ideology, the word in all its functions. A pure psychological or psychoanalytical reading of the story would not have been sufficient to illuminate all the aspects, as I have tried to do, even though briefly.

5 • What Would Happen If . . .

"HYPOTHESES ARE NETS," Novalis wrote. "You throw out your net, and sooner or later you catch something."

Here is a good example straight away: *What would happen if, upon awakening, a man found himself changed into a filthy cockroach?* The answer to this question can be found in Franz Kafka's story "The Metamorphosis." Of course, it was not this question that produced the story, but the form of the narrative certainly assumes the development of a pure fantastic hypothesis, including its tragic consequence. Within this hypothesis everything becomes logical and humane; everything is loaded with meaning open to various interpretations. The symbol leads an autonomous life and is applicable to many realities.

The technique of the "fantastical hypothesis" is extremely simple. It assumes its form precisely from the question: "What if?"

In order to form this question, any subject and predicate can be chosen haphazardly. The hypothesis that is to be elaborated is formed by linking the two together.

The subject could be "Reggio Emilia" and the predicate "to fly." *What if the city of Reggio Emilia were suddenly to fly?*

The subject could be "Milan" and the predicate "surrounded by water." *What if Milan were suddenly surrounded by water?*

Here are two situations within which the narrative events can multiply themselves spontaneously into infinity. In order to accumulate provisional material we can imagine the reactions of different people to the unusual news, incidents of every kind that take place, and the heated discussions. A choral story similar to the work of the Italian writer Palazzeschi. We can select a protagonist—for example, a boy—and let the adventures turn around him like a carousel of surprises.

I have noticed that children who live in the country, when confronted with this type of theme, attribute the first discovery of the news to the village baker because it is he who gets up before anyone else, even before the bell-ringer who is supposed to sound the church bells for early mass. In the city it is the night watchman who makes the discovery, and depending on whether the children have a stronger feeling for civil order or for family ties, they have the night watchman report the news to the mayor or to his wife.

City children are more or less compelled to let unknown people act. Country children are more fortunate. They are not compelled to think of a certain type like "the baker," but they think of the baker Giuseppe right away—(This name is obligatory for me; my father was a baker, and his name was Giuseppe)—and this helps them to introduce immediately people they know into the story, their relatives and friends. The game becomes more entertaining right away.

In the two articles that I mentioned in the preface, the ones published in *Paese sera*, I formulated the following questions:

- What would happen if everyone in Sicily lost their buttons?
- What would happen if a crocodile knocked on your door and asked for a little bit of rosemary?
- What would happen if your elevator plunged to the center of the earth or soared toward the moon?

It was only from the third theme that I later developed a story, using a young waiter in a cafe as the protagonist.

Children, too, take the greatest pleasure in asking the most comical and most surprising questions. This is precisely because the subsequent work, the development of the theme, is nothing more than the application and the unraveling of a discovery that has already taken place, provided that the theme—when it is a child's personal experience and includes his or her community and surroundings—lends itself to a direct intervention, an unusual appropriation of a reality that is loaded with meaning for the child.

Some time ago I worked with children in a middle school to formulate the following question: *What if a crocodile appeared as a contestant at a TV quiz show, winner take all?*

This question produced wonderful results. It provided a new perspective for watching television and for judging one's own experience with television. In the process some good things came of this. To begin with, there was a conversation with the crocodile, who wanted to be introduced as a specialist in ego-thology, and thus puzzled the TV announcer. During the actual quiz, the crocodile proved itself to be unbeatable. With each doubling of the prize, it ate its opponent without shedding a tear. In the end, it also ate the show's host, Mike Bongiorno, but it was then devoured in turn by the quiz master's assistant Sabina, whom the children greatly admired and wanted to see win no matter what.

Later I entirely rewrote this story and included it my book *Novelle fatte a macchina* (*Stories Told by a Machine*). In my story the crocodile is an expert on cat manure—fecal material if you will—but is very effective in lending the story a demythifying function. In the end, Sabina does not eat the crocodile, but compels it to spit out its victims in the reverse order that it had swallowed them.

It seems to me that the story does not concern nonsense. Rather it clearly deals with the use of the imagination to produce an active connection to reality.

The world can be looked at from the height of a man, but also from a cloud (airplanes have made this easy for us). Reality can be entered through the main door or it can be slipped into through a window, which is much more fun.

6 • Lenin's Grandfather

THIS CHAPTER is merely the continuation of the previous one. But I am too fond of the idea of bestowing a chapter title on Lenin's grandfather to give up the arbitrary caesura.

The country house of Lenin's grandfather was located not far from Kazan—the capital of the independent republic of Tatar—near the top of a small hill. At the foot of the hill was a little stream, a tributary of the Kolchose River, and ducks used to swim in it. It was a beautiful place, and some time ago I visited it and drank very good wine with my Tatar friends there.

One side of the living room had three windows that opened up to the garden. The children, among them Volodia Ulianov, the future Lenin, went in and out of the house through the windows rather than through the door. The wise Professor Blank (Lenin's grandfather on his mother's side) was very careful not to forbid this innocent fun and had firm benches placed beneath the windows so that the children could go in and out without the danger of breaking their necks. It seemed to me to be an exemplary way of placing oneself at the service of children's imagination.

By using stories and those fantastic methods that produce them, we help children to enter reality through the window instead of through the door. It is more fun. Therefore, it is more useful.

Moreover, there is nothing to prevent anyone from having an impact on reality by means of more demanding hypotheses.

For example: *What would happen if there were suddenly no more money to be found in the entire world, from the North Pole to the South?*

This is not just a theme for the imagination of children, which is exactly why I believe it to be an especially appropriate theme for children who take pleasure in measuring themselves by confronting problems that are greater than they are. It is the only means to grow that they have at their disposal. And there can be no doubt that, above all and more than anything else, they want to grow.

We recognize their right to grow, in fact, only with words. Each time, when they take us at our word, we risk our entire authority if we hinder them from growing.

To conclude I now want to point out that, in the final analysis, the fantastic hypothesis is nothing but a particular case of the fantastic binominal which originates from the arbitrary union of a certain subject with a certain predicate. It changes the components of the binominal, but not its function. In those general cases I described in the previous chapters, I examined the binominal, which consisted of two nouns. On the other hand, in the fantastic hypothesis, a noun and a verb, a subject and a predicate, or even a subject and an attribute come together.

Examples:

- noun and verb: "the city," "flies"
- subject and predicate: "Milan is surrounded by water"
- subject and attribute: "the crocodile," "expert on cat manure"

Of course, there can be other forms of fantastic hypotheses. But for the purpose of this book, these examples are sufficient.

7 • The Arbitrary Prefix

ONE WAY OF MAKING words productive in a fantastic sense is by deforming them. Children do it in their games. These games have a very serious content because they help children explore the possibilities of words, to master them, and to compel the words to assume new meanings. The games stimulate the children's freedom as "speakers" with a right to their personal *parole* (thank you, Monsieur Saussure). They encourage nonconformity.

The arbitrary prefix was developed in keeping with the spirit of these games, and I myself have frequently made good use of it.

It is sufficient to employ the prefix *de-* to transform the word *sharpener*—an everyday and negligible object, moreover dangerous and offensive—into a "desharpener," a fantastic and peaceful object. It is used not to sharpen pencils, but to allow the points of the pencils to grow back by themselves when they have become dull. Of course, this would enrage the owners of stationery stores and the ideological champions of consumerism. All this carries sexual innuendoes with it. Certainly, they are very much concealed, but they are not neglected by children (beneath the level of their consciousness).

The prefix *off-* generates *offrack*, the opposite of a rack for clothes. Here a person does not hang clothes on the rack, but takes them off whenever they are needed in order to get dressed. All this takes place in a country where the shop windows do not have glass, the stores are without cash registers, and the coat-checks are used without claim checks. From the prefix to utopia. But certainly it is not forbidden to imagine a city in the future where coats do not cost anything, like water and air. And utopia is not any less educational than the analytical spirit. It is sufficient to transfer utopia from the world of the intellect (that Antonio Gramsci justifiably aligned with methodical pessimism) to that of the will (whose principle characteristic, according to Gramsci, must be optimism). In sum, the clothes rack as such is only a "paper tiger."

Aside from this, I invented a country with *anti-*, where there is an anti-cannon with which war is not waged but rather hindered. The "sense of nonsense" (this expression was coined by Alfonso Gatto) is obvious in this case.

The prefix *bi-* gives us the "bi-pen," which writes everything doubly (and perhaps is useful for twin students). There is also the "bi-pipe" for smokers who want double pleasure, and the "Bi-Earth":

> There is a second Earth. We live on this one and that one at the same time. Everything that stands on its head here is on its feet there. And vice versa. Each one of us has his or her double there. (Science fiction has made ample use of similar hypotheses. This is why it also seems to me legitimate to speak about this with children.)

In an older story I introduced the "arch-dogs," the "arch-bones," and the "tri-noculars" (a product of the prefix *tri-*, as in "tri-cow," an animal unfortunately unknown to zoology).

In my archives I possess an "anti-umbrella," but I have not yet succeeded in imagining a practical use for it.

The prefix *de-* lends itself wonderfully to dismantling (*demontage*), with which it is easy to obtain the word *deassignment,* which means an assignment like homework that one does not have to do. Rather, it is to be destroyed or torn to pieces.

Returning to zoology to free it from the parentheses in which I left it, let us take up the "vicedog" and the "subcat." I shall give these animals as gifts to those people who need them to populate their stories.

Since I am handing out gifts, I shall give Italo Calvino, the author of *The Non-Existent Knight and the Cloven Viscount,* a "semighost," half-human made out of flesh and blood, and half-ghost in chains, covered by white sheets, that lends itself wonderfully to the invention of comical horror stories.

Superman already exists in the comics and is a striking example of the application of the principle of the "fantastic prefix" (even when it is a pure imitation of the "superman" of Nietzsche, the poor man). But if you want a "supergoaltender" or a "supermatch" (supposedly capable of setting the entire Milky Way aflame), you have only to fabricate it yourself.

Prefixes such as *micro-, mini-,* and *maxi-,* which emerged during the twentieth century, seem to me to be particularly productive. Here I offer—always without charge—a micro-hippopotamus (to be kept at home in an aquarium), a mini-skyscraper, to be kept in a mini-drawer and inhabited only by mini-millionaires, and a maxi-blanket, with which one can cover all the people in winter so that they do not freeze.

It is probably superfluous to point out that the fantastic prefix is also nothing else but a particular case of the fantastic binominal with the following components: the prefix chosen to produce new images, and the traditional word chosen to be changed and graced by the deformation.

If I were to suggest an exercise here, I would advise writing two parallel columns of arbitrarily chosen prefixes and nouns on a blackboard and then joining them together through the drawing of lots. I tried this. Ninety-nine percent of those marriages arranged according to this rite fail, but the hundredth turns out to be a happy and productive couple.

8 · The Creative Error

A STORY CAN ARISE from a slip of the hand. There is nothing new about this. Sometimes, when I am typing an article, I make interesting mistakes. For instance, once I typed "Lampland" instead of "Lapland," and by doing this I discovered a new country with its own special aroma and woods. It would be a sin to banish it from the map of possibilities with an eraser. It would be better to explore it like a tourist of the imagination.

If a child writes in his or her notebook "Atlantis Ocean" instead of "Atlantic Ocean," I can either correct this error with a red or blue pencil or follow the bold inspiration and write about the history and geography of this highly important body of water, marked on the map of the world. Will the moon be reflected on its surface?

A magnificent example of the creative error can be found, according to Stith Thompson (*The Folktale*), in *Cinderella* by Charles Perrault: the slipper, which in the original oral tradition was supposed to be made out of fur (*vaire*), was changed by chance into glass (*verre*). A glass slipper is certainly more fantastic than a fur slipper and also much more appealing, even if it stemmed from wordplay or from an error in transcription.

The orthographic error, if carefully considered, can give rise to all sorts of comical and instructive stories. Such stories can also have an ideological aspect, as I have endeavored to show in my book *Libro degli errori* (*Book of Errors*). In Italian, to write *Italia* with a *g* in the middle, *Itaglia*, may not just be due to the sloppiness of a student. In fact, there are people who scream and accentuate "I-ta-glia, I-ta-glia," with an ugly additional *g*, endowing it with a nationalistic and fascist tone. Italia does not need an additional *g*, but rather honest and decent people, and if it needs anything at all, then it needs intelligent revolutionaries.

9 · Old Games

THE SEARCH FOR the fantastic motif occurs in games cultivated by the dadaists and surrealists, but these games are certainly older than these movements. We may call them surrealist practices more out of convenience than as a somewhat belated homage to André Breton.

One of these games consists of clipping out headlines from newspapers and mixing them to obtain news about absurd, sensational, or simply amusing events:

The steeple of St. Peter
Wounded after a fight
Flees with the money to Switzerland

Bad accident on the highway
Between two tangos
In honor of George Washington

It is possible to compose entire poems using a newspaper and a pair of scissors, even though these poems may not make any sense. And yet there will be a fascinating sense.

I do not want to maintain that this is the most useful method for reading a newspaper or that newspapers should be used in schools only to be cut into pieces. Paper is something to be taken seriously. Likewise, the freedom of the press. This game is not intended to bring about disrespect for the printed word, although it can serve to temper the worship of the press as a sacred institution. In the final analysis, the invention of stories is to be taken seriously.

The unusual events that result from the activity I have described can continually generate comic effects or beginnings that can be developed into a true and proper narrative. It seems to me that every single mode of exploring coincidence is good. Technically, the game drives the process of estranging the words to their utmost extremes and produces genuine chains of fantastic binominals. In this case we should perhaps look upon them as fantastic polynominals.

Another old game known throughout the world is the question-and-answer routine using slips of paper. It begins with a series of questions that already include a sequence of events. In other words, the sequence contains the form of a narration:

1) Who was it?
2) Where was he?
3) What did he do?
4) What did he say?
5) What did the people say?
6) What happened in the end?

The first child in the group answers the first question and folds his slip so that nobody can read the answer. The second child responds to the second question and also folds his slip of paper. The game continues this way until there are no more questions. Then the children read the answers aloud like a story. The answers can lead to total nonsense or produce the seeds of a comical story. For example:

A dead man
on the leaning tower of Pisa
sewed socks.
He said: how much is three times three?
The people sang the national anthem
and it ended three to zero.

This story originated truly by chance. In the game, the children read the answers aloud. They have a good laugh, and that is the end of it. Or, the situation that arises from the answers can be analyzed and developed into a story.

Basically, this game is the same as selecting a motif through random words. The essential difference is that a "coincidental syntax" is chosen through this process. Instead of a fantastic binominal, there is a fantastic plot. By varying and complicating the questions, highly stimulating results can be obtained.

Another famous surrealist game can also lead to exciting results when different participants draw pictures together. The first child in the group draws a figure, depicts a scene, or traces a sign that may or may not have a meaning. The second, in each case, does not pay attention to the meaning but uses the symbol of the first child as an element of another figure with a different meaning. The third child does the same thing, not to complete the drawing of the first two children but rather to change its direction, to turn it another way. The final result is frequently enough an incomprehensible drawing that does not have a set form. On the contrary, the forms fuse with one another in a kind of perpetual motion.

I have seen children amuse themselves a great deal by playing this game, and they quickly learn its rules. For example, one child draws the oval of an eye. The second, who gives the oval another meaning, adds the feet of a chicken to it. The third has a flower spring from the position of the head. Et cetera. The final product is less important than the struggle to master the forms of others and to impose one's own; the product is less important than the surprises and the discoveries that occur at each step in a movement that Umberto Eco might call "the fluctuation of meaning."

At the end, however, the figures can contain a story. An unusual character can unexpectedly appear, or perhaps a monster or a fantastic landscape. At this point the words can continue the game. The movement is once again from nonsense to sense. The stimulus for the imagination is born in this game from the intuition of a new connection between two elements that chance places in contact with one another. They can be—to borrow the jargon of the linguists—"forms of expression" or "forms of content" that are articulated in different ways, but the binominal rhythm remains at the bottom of their changes. The realm of dialectics also extends itself into the terrain of the imagination.

10 · How Limericks Are Made

THE LIMERICK is an organized and codified genre of nonsense. Among the more famous limericks are those by Edward Lear. For example,

There was once an Old Man in a Marsh,
Whose manners were futile and harsh;
He sat on a Log,

And sang Songs to a Frog,
That instructive Old Man in a Marsh.

With very few variations, all limericks have always used the same structure, which has been analyzed with great precision by the Soviet semioticians Civian and Segal.

The first line indicates the protagonist—the old man in a marsh. The second line points out his characteristics—futile and harsh. The third and fourth lines realize the actions of the protagonist—he sits on a log and sings songs to a frog. The fifth line is reserved for the final point or epithet that is to be appropriately extravagant.

Some variants are really alternative forms of the same structure. For example, in the second line, the person's characteristics can be indicated by an object that the protagonist possesses rather than by his or her own qualities, or by an action that he or she carries out. In the third and fourth lines the reactions of the other people can be presented rather than the actions of the protagonist. In the fifth line the protagonist can experience a retaliation (reprisal) more serious than a simple epithet.

Let us look at another example from Lear.

1) *the protagonist*
   There once was an old Man of Melrose
2) *the attributes*
   Who walked on the tips of his toes;
3 & 4) *the reaction of the others*
   But they said "It ain't pleasant,
   To see you at present,
5) *final epithet*
   You stupid old Man of Melrose."

If we recast this structure—that is, if we use it as a true and proper guide for the composition of a poem and respect the combination of the rhymes (the first, second and fifth lines rhyme with one another; the third line rhymes with the fourth)—then we can compose our own "limerick" in the same manner as Lear.

First step: choice of a protagonist
   1) A tiny man from Rome
Second step: indication of a quality expressed through an action
   2) Went up the stairs of a dome.
Third step: reaction of the others
   3/4) When he reached the high spot

> He was still just a dot
> *Fourth step: final epithet*
> 5) The mini-man from Rome.

Another example from Lear:

There was once an Old Man in a Garden
Who always begged everyone's pardon.
> When they asked him, "What for?"
> He replied, "You're a bore!
And I trust you'll go out of my garden."

In this case the last line is not an epithet but brings about a contradiction of the polite old man in the garden. The rhymes are not pure. But I believe that, when it comes to fabricating nonsense, there is no place for pedantry. The structure of the limerick has been recast only because it is easy. When tried and tested, it leads infallibly to a result, but not the way a homework assignment is carried out.

Children need but a short time to learn the technique described here. It is particularly amusing to search for the final epithet with them. It can be a made-up or imaginative word, an invented adjective, with one foot in grammar and the other in parody. Many limericks make do with less. But children place great stock in the epithet. Here is an example:

A man by the name of Mark
Loved to hear concerts in the park.
He ate horned crumpets
While listening to trumpets
Our lover of music, Mister Mark.

The epithet "lover of music" is nothing special. In fact, after hearing this limerick, a boy drew my attention to the fact that it would be more appropriate to call Mister Mark a music hater because he ate horned crumpets while listening to music. And he was right.

Another critic—this time an adult, not a child—told me that the limericks I had made were not truly "nonsensical," even if they did contain stories that could be called absurd. He, too, was right. But I didn't know what to do. My difficulty may result from the difference between English and Italian. Or it may result from our tendency to rationalize.

In the interest of children, it is important not to limit the possibilities of the absurd. I do not believe that such possibilities are detrimental to their education in science. Besides, even in mathematics there are formulas to "demonstrate the absurd."

11 • How Riddles Are Made

IS THE INVENTION of a riddle an exercise in logic or in the imagination? Probably both at the same time. The rule of this exercise stems from the analysis of one of the more simple popular riddles in Italian folklore. It was told in the following manner when water wells were still in use.

"What goes down laughing and comes back up crying?"

"A bucket."

At the root of this concealed definition, there is a process of estrangement of the object. The bucket becomes separated from its meaning and customary context when it is simply described as an object that descends and ascends.

In the description, however, there are penetrating associations and comparisons that no longer concern the whole object but one of its features, namely its musical aspect. The bucket clatters. But the clattering noise is different when it is sent down the well and when it is pulled up with water in it. The key to the new definition is in the metaphor that originates from the verb *to cry*. When the bucket is pulled up, it sways, and the water drips out. The bucket "cries." It rises crying. And it is from this metaphor that the first one originates in opposition. "Laughing it goes down." Now the double metaphor is ready to represent the object, to conceal it, and to elevate it from a banal, daily utensil to a mysterious object that challenges the imagination.

Here the analysis offers us the following sequence: "estrangement-association-metaphor." These are the three steps necessary to arrive at forming the riddle. We can test these rules with any object whatsoever. For example, a pen (which today would more than likely be a ballpoint pen rather than a fountain pen).

First step: estrangement. We must define the pen as though we were seeing it for the first time. It is a little stick made mainly out of plastic in the form of a cylinder or a multifaceted pipe, terminating with a pointed cone. When it is rubbed on a clear surface, it leaves a visible mark behind.

Second step: association and comparison. The "clear surface" of the definition opens up the way for other meanings through images. The sheet of white paper can become any other white surface, such as a wall or a field covered with snow. By analogy, what is a "black mark" on a white sheet can become a "black path on a white field."

Third step: the final metaphor. We are now ready for a metaphorical definition of the pen: "Something that makes a black path on a white field."

Fourth step: though not essential, this step consists in giving an appropriate form to the mysterious definition. The riddles are frequently formed in verse. In our case it is easy:

What's black and needs white
to make its mark look bright?

It is important to emphasize the crucial importance of the first step, which seems merely to be a preparatory one. In reality, the estrangement is an essential moment that makes the least banal associations possible and permits the sudden flash of the most surprising metaphors which, for the person guessing, are more exciting than an obscure stimulus.

Why do children like riddles so much? My hunch is that it is because they represent the concentrated form—and are somewhat emblematical—of their experience of conquering reality. For a child, the world is full of mysterious objects, incomprehensible events, and indecipherable figures. Their own presence in the world is a mystery to be resolved, a riddle to solve, and they circle around it with direct or indirect questions.

Hence their pleasure derives from an objective manner of testing through play, somewhat like training the emotions to feel the excitement of the search and surprise.

If my hunch is right, the game of hide and seek also has something to do with the pleasure that children have with riddles. However, the riddle has a different principal content: that of reliving, as a test, the fear of being abandoned, of being lost. Or of losing oneself. Yes, it is little Tom Thumb who plays at losing himself in the woods. To be found is like returning to the world, reacquiring one's own rights, being born again. I did not exist before this. Now I am here. I no longer exist. Here I am again.

In these challenges, children's feelings of security are reinforced, their capacity to grow, their pleasure in existing and knowing.

Much more can be said about all this, but this would be beyond the scope of my present project.

12 • Popular Folk Tales as Raw Material

POPULAR FOLK TALES have entered imaginative writing from the oral tradition as raw material: they have made their way from the literary game (Gianfranco Straparola) to the courtly game (Charles Perrault); from romanticism to positivism. Finally, in our century, the great accomplishments of fantastic philology permitted Italo Calvino to provide the Italian language with what it had not received in the nineteenth century, due to the fact that no Italian Grimm existed at that time. Here I shall keep quiet about all those imitations that damaged the tales as well as the pedagogical distortions and the commercial exploitation (Disney) they have suffered.

Fortunately, Hans Christian Andersen and Carlo Collodi were inspired by the popular tradition of folk tales even though the two of them took different paths.

Like the Brothers Grimm, Andersen took the popular tales of his country as his starting point. But the Grimms, those stalwart Germans, were interested in constructing a living monument to the German language in a Germany that Napoleon had subjugated. They accomplished this by transcribing tales told to them by common storytellers (an undertaking that earned them recognition as patriots from the Prussian Minister of Education). In contrast, Andersen revived folk tales from memory: they were merely a means for him to approach his childhood again and to redeem it, not to give voice to his people. "I and the fairy tale" was the fantastic binominal that served his work as the ultimate constellation. Then Andersen broke away from the traditional folk tale to create a new fairy tale, populated with romantic characters and everyday objects, even filled with personal feelings of revenge. His reading of folk and fairy tales, which had been radiated by the "romantic sun," so to speak, helped him to free his imagination completely and to master his language sufficiently so that he could speak to children without becoming childish.

On the other hand, Collodi's *Pinocchio* took its life from the Tuscan landscape, from the tones and colors of Tuscan folklore. The Tuscan folk tales provided Collodi's narrative with a profound substratum of raw material, but the folklore was only one of the elements of raw material in the language, for the raw material is somewhat complex, as one can perceive *a posteriori* from the different interpretations that *Pinocchio* has received and continues to receive.

The Brothers Grimm, Andersen, and Collodi—with regard to fairy tales—have been among the great liberators of children's literature, freeing it from the pedagogical tasks that were assigned to it as public schools began to be established. (In the domain of "adventure," pioneers and explorers, the avant garde of colonialism, have revealed themselves to be valuable allies of children, along with pirates, corsairs, and other rough characters.)

It is possible to view Andersen as the first creator of the contemporary fairy tale: themes and characters of the past leave their limbo, which is no longer timeless, to act in the purgatory or the hell of the present. Collodi went even further by giving children—as they are and not as their teachers or ministers want them to be—the role of the protagonist and by assigning new roles to certain characters of the classical fairy tale: Collodi's girl with the dark blue hair (later the fairy) is only a distant relative of the traditional fairies. The old ogre can be recognized again in the dress of the Fire-eater or the Green Fisherman; the little Butterball is a slight caricature of the magician.

Andersen cannot be surpassed in the way he animates the most banal objects, providing the best possible examples of how to bring about "estrangement" and "amplification." Collodi's dialogues cannot be surpassed. He had trained himself by writing bad comedies for many years.

Neither Andersen nor Collodi—and this demonstrates that they were brilliant writers—knew the fairy tale material the way we know it today—catalogued, dissected, and studied under the psychological, psychoanalytical, formal, anthropological, and structural microscope, et cetera. As a result, we are now in a position to "treat" classical fairy tales as an entire series of fantastic games, and in the following chapters, I shall say something about these games, just as it occurs to me, without ordering the games into a system.

13 • Making Mistakes in the Story

"ONCE UPON A TIME there was a girl who was called Little Yellow Riding Hood."

"No, Little *Red* Riding Hood!"

"Ah yes. Little Red Riding Hood. Well then, her father called her. . . ."

"No, not her father, her mother."

"Right. She called her and said to her: Go to Aunt Rosina and take her. . . ."

"Go to grandmother, she told her, not to her aunt!"

Et cetera.

This is the outline of an old game, "Making Mistakes in the Story," that can be created at any time in any home. I adapted it many years ago in my book, *Favole al telefono* (*Telephone Tales*).

It is a more serious game than it seems at first sight. But it must be played at the right time. When it comes to fairy tales, young children tend to be conservative. They want to hear the tales time and again with the same words as the first time, because they take pleasure in recognizing them again, in learning them in the proper sequence from beginning to end, in testing their emotions from their first encounter in the same order: surprise, fear, gratification. They need order and reassurance: the world should not leave the tracks so brusquely on which they move forward with such a great effort.

Therefore, it is possible that children will initially become irritated when the game of making mistakes is played, because they feel threatened. They are prepared for the appearance of the wolf. But the appearance of something new unsettles them because they do not know whether it is a friend or a foe.

At a certain point—perhaps when *Little Red Riding Hood* no longer has much to say to them, when they are ready to distance themselves from the tale just as they separate from an old toy that has been all used up—they are willing to accept a parody of the story. They will accept this in part because parody sanctions the distance that they take, but also in part because the new viewpoint renews their interest in the story itself, revives the story, and takes off on another track. The children are no longer playing so much with *Little Red Riding Hood*, but with themselves: they dare themselves to face freedom without fear and to assume risks and responsibility. Therefore, it is necessary to be prepared for a healthy overdose of aggression, for excessive leaps into the absurd.

If this is the case, the game will have its therapeutic effect. It will help children to free themselves from certain fixations. The game de-dramatizes the wolf, scolds the monster, makes the witch ridiculous, stabilizes a little more clearly the boundary between the world of real things—where certain liberties are not possible—and the world of fantastic things. This must happen sooner or later, but certainly not before the wolf, the monster, and the witch have fulfilled their deep functions, but it must also not happen too late.

Another serious aspect of the game demands that the participants produce a genuine and original analysis of the fairy tale on an intuitive level. The alternatives or the parodies can be initiated and developed only at certain points and not at others—and these are the precise points that characterize and structure the fairy tale—not during its tranquil verbal shifts from one node of meaning to another. The processes of decomposition and recomposition are simultaneous in this game. This is exactly why they are operative interventions, and not abstract and logical.

The result of all this is a "pointed" invention that rarely leads to a new synthesis with a new logic. Instead it favors a kind of wandering among the fairy tale motifs without a precise goal. It is more doodling than drawing. Nowadays, however, we know the usefulness of doodling.

14 • Little Red Riding Hood in a Helicopter

IN SOME SCHOOLS that I have visited, I have observed the following game. The children are given some words, which they use to make a story. For example, a series of five words that suggest the tale of *Little Red Riding Hood*: girl, woods, flowers, wolf, grandmother. The sixth word breaks the series. For example, helicopter.

The teachers or the other people who conduct this experiment, a game-exercise, seek to measure the capacity of the children to react to a new and unexpected element introduced into a certain series of events; their capacity to absorb the given word in the familiar story; and their capacity to make the familiar words react in the new context in which they find themselves.

Upon closer examination, the game has the form of a fantastic binominal. On the one hand, there is Little Red Riding Hood; on the other, the helicopter. The second part of the binominal is a single word. However, the first part is a series of words that combine and form a unit to confront the word *helicopter*. From the viewpoint of the logic of the fantastic, everything is thus clear.

In my opinion, the most interesting results produced by this game are for psychologists, when this fantastic theme is given cold, without preparation and also without a great deal of explanation.

After I first learned about this experiment from a teacher in Viterbo—whose name and address I have unfortunately lost—I tried it out with some children in the second grade whose minds had been blocked by a teaching routine of the worst kind (dictation, copying, and other similar things). In other words, they were being taught under terrible conditions. I attempted in vain to draw a story out of them. This is a difficult undertaking when a stranger suddenly appears in the midst of children and nobody knows what he wants. Moreover, I only had a few minutes at my disposal because I was expected in other classes. But I was sorry to leave the children without having done anything except to give them the memory of an eccentric guy who played the clown by sitting on the ground and climbing on top of a chair (necessary moves on my part to break the bureaucratic atmosphere created by the presence of the teacher and the school inspector). If I had only brought with me a harmonica, a flute, or a drum. . . .

Finally, it occurred to me to ask if any of them wanted to tell the story of *Little Red Riding Hood*. The girls pointed to a boy, the boys to a girl.

"And now," I asked the children, after the boy had finished rattling off the story to me, not actually the story of *Little Red Riding Hood* as his grandmother had probably told him, but an insipid litany (which sounded like a school recital, the poor child)—"and now, give me any word that comes to your mind."

But they did not grasp what I meant by "any word." I had to explain it to them. Finally, they gave me the word *horse.* I could now tell them the story of Little Red Riding Hood who met a horse in the woods. She climbed on his back and got to her grandmother's house before the wolf. . . .

Right after this I went to the blackboard, and as the room was filled with attentive silence and the children were burning with curiosity, I wrote: girl, woods, flowers, wolf, grandmother, helicopter. . . . I turned around. I did not have to explain the new game to anyone. The minds of the brightest children had already clicked, and they raised their hands. With many voices they produced a nice story: the wolf, when he knocks at grandmother's door, is observed by the police from a helicopter. "What is he doing there? What does he want?" the policemen ask. And they descend in time to drive the wolf into the arms of the hunter. . . .

One can debate the ideological value of the new creation, but this does not appear to me to be the point. What is more important is what was set in motion. I am certain that these children will ask every now and then to play the game of Little Red Riding Hood again with a new word: they will get to know the pleasure of inventing.

An experiment of invention is wonderful when the children enjoy themselves, even when they break the rules of the experiment itself to arrive at the goal, for the children are the goal.

15 • The Fairy Tale Reversed

ONE VARIANT in the game of making mistakes in the fairy tale consists of a premeditated and purposeful reversal of the fairy tale theme:

Little Red Riding Hood is bad, and the wolf is good. . . .

Tom Thumb wants to escape from home with his brothers and abandon their poor parents. However, the parents are aware of this. So Tom and his brothers fill their pockets with rice and make holes in them so that they will be able to determine their path of escape. (As in the original tale, but everything is turned upside down. Where the right side was, we now see the left. . . .)

Cinderella is so very bad that she drives her patient stepmother to despair and steals her stepsisters' fiancés.

Instead of dwarfs, Snow White encounters seven giants in the woods, where it is most dense and dark. She becomes their mascot and helps them commit criminal acts.

The technique of making mistakes creates guidelines for itself, a projected plan. The result is partially or totally new depending on whether the "reversal" includes one or all the elements of the particular fairy tale.

Through the "reversal" we can also attain stories other than a parody. For example, the reversal can be the starting point for an independent story that develops automatically in another direction.

A child in the fourth grade who was especially creative played with real history and historical legends instead of making use of the technique of reversing fairy tales. Remus kills Romulus; the new city is called Rema not Rome; and its inhabitants are called Remans. With the new name "Remans," the Romans no longer terrify people. Instead, the Romans as Remans are figures of ridicule. So, Hannibal defeats the Remans and becomes Emperor of Rema. Et cetera.

The exercise does not have any historical relevance because it is not made from "if," so to speak. Moreover, the exercise takes more from Voltaire than from Borges. It is possible that the result of the exercise is more appreciable, even if it is involuntary, because it parodies the manner, or the pretext, of teaching Roman history to children in the elementary schools.

16 • What Happens After?

"AND AFTER?" the children ask when the narrator stops.

Even when a fairy tale is finished, there is always the possibility of an "after." The characters are ready to act. We know how they relate to one another. The simple introduction of a new element sets the entire internal mechanism in motion once again, as all those writers who have written or conceived a sequel to *Pinocchio* certainly know.

A group of children from a fifth grade class took a remarkable "step backward" and introduced a new element directly into the belly of the shark. (In the original Italian fairy tale novel by Collodi, the Disney whale is really a shark.) On this very day—it is the day that Pinocchio becomes a real boy—Geppetto suddenly remembers that he had seen a hidden treasure in the belly of the monster during the time of his imprisonment. Pinocchio immediately organizes a hunt for the shark, which is simultaneously a hunt for the treasure. But he is not the only one. Indeed, the Green Fisherman, who has in the meantime become a pirate, is also searching for the treasure that he has heard about from the Cat and the Fox, who now form his crew, as improbable as that may seem. After many adventurous encounters, Pinocchio triumphs in the end. But the ending has an epilogue: the shark, caught and stuffed, is publicly displayed in shows put on by Geppetto, who is now too old to be a carpenter, but not too old to collect and tear the admission tickets.

The fantastic binomial that governs the movement of the new story is "Pinocchio-hidden treasure." To be exact, it is the same story, but it reinstates the hero after he failed to reap a treasure when he was still a puppet, and naïvely sowed gold coins as seeds to see if he could grow a plant from them.

There is a famous parody sequel to *Cinderella*, too. (But does it really exist? At any rate I remember it, and I don't think I invented it.) After Cinderella has married Prince Charming, she keeps her old habits as guardian of home and hearth, a veritable housewife, always with an apron, unkempt and uncombed. After a few weeks the prince can only be bored by such a wife as this. Cinderella's stepsisters are much more entertaining and attractive. They love dances, the cinema, cruises to the Caribbean Islands. The same stepmother, who is still young and has many different interests (she plays the piano, goes to lectures about the Third World, and to literary circles), cannot be discounted. A tragedy ensues due to jealousy, with all the gory details printed in the newspapers. . . .

The crux of the game consists of a fresh analysis of the fairy tale on an intuitive level. The structures of the fairy tale are played with in such a manner that one of the motifs is given preference over the others. In the fairy tale about Cinderella, her situation as guardian of the hearth is a condemnation. In the sequel, this motif is expanded into a gigantic caricature that compels the other motifs, such as the motif of the mundane stepsisters, to assume new meanings.

If the fairy tale about Little Tom Thumb is told to a group of children, it may happen that one child will ask at the end of the story, "And what did Tom Thumb do afterwards with the seven-league boots?" Of all the motifs in this fairy tale, it is this one that strikes this child most of all and stimulates him or her to think up a sequence. It is an example of the "privileging of a motif."

If among all the motifs present in *Pinocchio*, we privilege the motif of the nose that grows longer with each lie, we can easily produce a new fairy tale in which Pinocchio intentionally lies in order to obtain heaps of wood to barter and sell. He becomes rich, and a monument is then erected in his honor during his lifetime. Made of wood, of course.

In the examples that I have cited, something intervenes like a "force of inertia" of the imagination that tends to persevere in its movement, transforming itself into automatic fantasizing. The new fairy tale, however, does not emanate from this automation, rather from its rationalization—that is, from the capacity to recognize a direction, a constructive impulse, that arises from the uncontrolled movement. Even in the best writing experiments of the surrealists, automaticism was repeatedly repudiated by an irresistible tendency of the imagination toward syntax.

17 • The Fairy Tale Salad

LITTLE RED RIDING HOOD encounters Little Tom Thumb and his brothers in the woods. Their adventures become mixed together, and they choose a new path that runs diagonally to both forces that act on the same point as in the famous parallelogram that I gaped at as it took shape on a blackboard in 1930 traced by the hands of my teacher Mr. Ferrari in Laveno.

He was a slender man with a little blond beard and glasses, and he had a limp. One time he gave an A to my rival in Italian for his essay. Even today I remember what this student wrote: "Humanity is more in need of good men than great men." It is clear from this that my teacher was a socialist. Another time he wanted to embarrass me and make clear to my schoolmates that I did not possess the key to all knowledge. So he said, "If I ask Gianni, for example, what 'beautiful' is in Latin, he will not know." But since I had heard "Tota pulchra es Maria" sung in church and I had been given to understand what those glorious words meant, I stood up and said with a blush, "It's *pulchra.*"

Everyone laughed, even the teacher, and I realized that it is not always necessary to say all that one knows. This is also why, in this book, I am abstaining as much as possible from using the difficult words that I know. When above I wrote the word *parallelogram,* which seems difficult, I remembered that I had learned it in fifth grade.

If Pinocchio were to land in the house of the seven dwarfs, he would be the eighth among the wards of Snow White. He would introduce his vital energy into the old story, compel it to recast itself according to the dictates of two rules, that of Pinocchio and that of Snow White.

The same thing occurs when Cinderella marries Bluebeard, when Puss in Boots places himself at the service of Hansel and Gretel, et cetera.

Subjected to this treatment, even the images that are most constantly used appear to take on a new life, to blossom again, and to bear fruit and flowers in unexpected ways. The hybrid has its fascination.

An inkling of this "fairy tale salad" can be noted in certain children's drawings in which the characters of different fairy tales live together in a fantastic manner. Indeed, I know a woman who made use of this technique when her children were young and continually longed to hear stories. As they grew older and asked for new stories, she improvised by mixing the characters from the old stories. She had the children themselves determine the theme. It is from her that I heard a grotesque mystery story in which the Prince, who woke Snow White from her sleep, was the same one who had married Cinderella the day before. An intense and scary drama developed out of this situation with terrible battles among the dwarfs, step-sisters, fairies, witches, and queens.

The type of fantastic binominal that governs this game distinguishes itself from the general form only because it is constituted by two proper nouns and not by two common nouns (a subject and a predicate, et cetera) as we saw before. Naturally, here *the proper nouns are taken from fairy tales*, a genre that the normal grammars are not obliged to note. It is as if "Snow White" and "Pinocchio" were the same as "Bill" and "Jane."

18 • Recasting Fairy Tales

THUS FAR the focus of the games has been old fairy tales. I have used their names openly and freely, and adopted their characters without re-baptizing them, even when their functions have been reversed and distorted in interesting ways. Their motifs have been remixed, and the force of inertia of their events has been exploited, but they were not torn out of their natural habitat.

A more complex game that I call recasting enables a new fairy tale to arise from an old one with various degrees of recognizability, or with a total transference to foreign terrain. There are famous precedents for this process. The most notable one was James Joyce's recasting of *The Odyssey*. But it is also not difficult to recognize the Greek myth in *The Erasers* by Alain Robbe-Grillet, and through close examination, we can rediscover the design of biblical stories in the plots of some works by Alberto Moravia. These examples have obviously nothing to do with the infinite number of plots in novels that spring from a simple change of names and transposition of the calendar.

The Odyssey serves Joyce only as a complex system of fantastic coordinates—a network in which he captures the reality of his Dublin, and at the same time it is a system of convex mirrors that reveals how dense this reality is that may otherwise escape the naked eye. Reduced to a game, the process does not lose its elegance and its capacity to excite.

A fairy tale can be reduced to the bare plot of its events and their internal relations.

> Cinderella lives with her stepmother and stepsisters who go to a grand ball and leave her at home. Through the intervention of a fairy, she, too, goes to the ball. The prince falls in love with her. Et cetera.

The second step consists in reducing the plot to a pure abstract expression:

> A lives in the house of B and stands in a relationship to B, different from the relationship that C and D have with B. While B, C, and D go to E, where there is some kind of event F, A remains alone. However, thanks to the intervention of G, A, too, is able to go to E and makes an extraordinary impression on H. Et cetera.

If we now interpret the abstract expression in a new way, we can obtain, for example, the following scheme:

> Delfina is the poor relative of Mrs. Notable, owner of a dry cleaning store in Boston, and the mother of two pretentious girls who still attend high school. While Mrs. Notable and her daughters take a rocket cruise to Mars, where a great intergalactic party is taking place, Delfina stays in the dry cleaning shop, ironing the evening gown of Lady Importanzia. Delfina tries it on and begins to fantasize about the ball. She goes into the street and jumps into Space Ship II without thinking about what she is doing. Indeed, it is the very spaceship in which Lady Importanzia is flying to the party on Mars, with Delfina as a stowaway. At the ball, the President of the Republic of Mars notices Delfina and dances with her. Et cetera.

In this example, the second step—the abstract formula of a particular fairy tale—appears almost superfluous due to the fact that the new plot recasts the first one, staying close to the original, and introducing simple variants. Almost superfluous, but not entirely, because in each case it has created a certain distance from the fairy tale, preparing its changeability.

After we have obtained the formula for forgetting the original fairy tale, we can arrive at the following:

> Carlo is a stable boy at the estate of Count Cindertolis, father of William and Anne. It is vacation time, and the count and his children decide to take a journey around the world in their yacht. Carlo slips secretly on board with the help of the cabin boy. The yacht, however, is shipwrecked on a primitive island where Carlo proves himself to be valuable by giving a cigarette lighter

as a present to the medicine man, who is the head of the natives. Carlo is celebrated as the god of fire. Et cetera.

With this story we have sufficiently distanced ourselves from the original character of Cinderella, who penetrates the new story like a woven secret, to experience her innermost feelings and inspirations of unthinkable developments. Seeing is believing, according to the old folk saying.
Another example:

Hansel and Gretel are brother and sister. They get lost in the forest. A witch takes them into her house, intending to bake them in her oven.

Let us recast the plot:

A and B get lost in the place C. They are taken by D into the place E, where there is also an oven F. . . .

And here we have the new plot:

A brother and sister (probably children from southern Italy who have emigrated north) have been abandoned by their father near the main cathedral in Milan. He is desperate because he cannot feed them and hopes they will be helped by public charity. But the children leave the cathedral and wander through the city. At night they take refuge in a courtyard, and they sleep beneath a pile of empty cartons. By chance a baker discovers them, and he takes them inside his shop where they enjoy the warmth of his oven. . . .

If I ask myself at which point a spark was ignited and my energy was set into motion to conceive the new story, I can easily respond that it was with the word *oven*. I have already said that I am the son of a baker. A baker's shop is usually associated with something to eat. To me, the word oven means a large room filled with sacks of flour and a mechanical mixer on the left-hand side. In front are the white tiles of the oven with the door that opens and shuts. My father, who kneads the flour, puts it in the oven and takes it out. Every day he made a dozen rolls from a white flour for me and my brother. These rolls were very crisp, and we devoured them like gluttons.

The last picture I have of my father is that of a man who tried in vain to warm his back on the oven. He was drenched and trembling. He had left the shop during a storm to help a little cat stranded between large puddles of water. Seven days later my father died of pneumonia. Penicillin had not yet been invented.

Later, when my father lay dead on his bed with his hands folded, I was led in to see him. I remember his hands but not his face. I also remember the man who warmed himself against the warm tiles of the oven, and I remember his arms, not his face. He had scorched the hair off his arms with a burning newspaper so that the hair would not fall onto the bread dough. The newspaper was *La gazzetta del popolo* (*The People's Gazette*). I know this for sure because it had a children's page. It was 1929.

The word *oven* had been swimming about in my memory, and it surfaced with sad and warm colors. These colors influenced the formation of the various unions in the tale—between the abandoned children of the fairy tale and those of the new one, between the trees of the forests and the pillars of the cathedral in Milan. The rest is deduction, fantastical not logical.

The story will have an unexpected ending because the baker bakes bread—not the children—in the oven. What is also unexpected is that the story invites us to look at the large industrial city from the lower depths, with the eyes of the two lost children, to discover the reality of a social drama in a game of the imagination. The contemporary world with all its violence will be entered through the abstract recasting: A, B, C, D. . . . We find ourselves once again on Earth, at the heart of the Earth. And in the recasting, political and ideological contents of a certain sign will make their mark because I am I, not an aristocratic lady of San Vincenzo. All of this happens inevitably. And as it happens, it produces images and signs that will need to be examined and interpreted in their turn.

The recasting usually offers different people different ways that lead to different "messages." But we did not start with the message. It emerged by itself as an involuntary point of arrival.

The essential moment of the "recasting" is the analysis of the given fairy tale. It is a process that is at once analytical and synthetic, and it goes from the concrete to the abstract, and from the abstract it turns to the concrete.

The possibility for a process of this kind stems from the very nature of the fairy tale itself: from its structure, strongly characterized by the presence and repetition of certain constitutive elements that we can call "motifs." Vladimir Propp called them "functions." And now it is to Propp we must turn to become more conscious of our game and to produce new devices.

19 • The Cards of Propp

ONE TIME, while reading the Italian edition of *Scientific American*, I came across an article that shed light on a characteristic aspect of Leonardo da

Vinci's genius. This article maintained that Leonardo's genius consisted in his capacity to regard a machine not as a unique organism, not as an inimitable prototype, but as a totality of simple machines. And he was the first to do this.

Leonardo broke down the machines into elements or "functions." In this way he succeeded in studying the "function" of friction in isolation, for example, and this manner of dissection enabled him to conceive the round bearings, cone couplings, and stump cylinders that have only recently been manufactured for gyroscopes, and are indispensable for aeronautics.

Leonardo derived a great deal of pleasure from studies of this kind. A few years ago one of his drawings for a burlesque invention was discovered—a safety mechanism to break the fall of a man from a high place. You can see the man falling from an undisclosed place, and his fall is broken by a system of conical wedges connected to each other, and at the final point of the fall, by a wool ball whose resistance to the impact is controlled and regulated by one last wedge. Most likely, we must also attribute the invention of "useless" machines to Leonardo, those machines constructed out of play, out of fantasy, designed with a smile. They were, at the moment of their conception, opposed to the utilitarian norm of scientific-technical progress.

In much the same way that Leonardo broke down a machine into its functions, Vladimir Propp, the Soviet linguist, dissected the functions of the popular folk tale in his books *Morphology of the Folk Tale* and *The Transformation of the Magic Fairy Tale*.

Propp is also famous for his book *The Historical Roots of the Fairy Tale*, and justifiably so. In this work he develops a captivating and convincing theory, at least from a poetical perspective, that shows how the oldest core of a magical fairy tale can be traced back to initiatory rituals practiced in primitive societies. In other words, all that the fairy tales narrate—or, in terms of their transformations, all that the tales conceal—happened at one time in history. When children reached a certain stage, they were separated from their family and taken to the forest (like Little Tom Thumb, Hansel and Gretel, and Snow White), where the shaman (or medicine man) of the tribe, dressed in a manner to make the children fearful, set difficult and frequently deadly tasks for them. Usually the shaman's face was covered with a horrible mask (that immediately makes us think of magicians and witches). In the magic folk tales all the protagonists are confronted with such tasks when they set out on their journeys. The boys listened to the tribal myths and stories and were entrusted with weapons (the magic gifts, which in the fairy tales are given to the endangered hero by supernatural donors), and in the end they returned to their home, frequently with other names (the hero of the fairy tale also returns home and is frequently unknown). At this point they were mature enough to marry (as in the fairy tale, which concludes with a marriage celebration ninety-nine percent of the time).

The structure of the fairy tale repeats the structure of the ritual. And it is precisely from this observation that Propp (and not only Propp) conceived the theory according to which the fairy tale came into existence as the ancient rituals were declining, leaving behind them the magic folk tale of the oral tradition that eventually formed the basis for the literary fairy tale. In the course of centuries, storytellers continually betrayed the memory of the ritual and became more and more accustomed to serving the autonomous exigencies of the magic folk tale spread by word of mouth. The magic folk tale accumulated variants, followed people (Indo-Europeans) in their migrations, and absorbed the effects of historical and social change. Thus, in the course of a few centuries, storytellers transformed a labile language and gave life to a new language. How much time has passed since the Latin of the old Roman Empire was transformed into the romance languages?

In sum, the fairy tales accordingly were born from the fall of the sacred world into a secular one—as though they tumbled into the world of children and were reduced to little toys, objects that in the preceding epochs had been ritual and cultural objects. For example, the same can be said of dolls or spinning tops. And wasn't the same process, the movement from the sacred to the profane, the formative basis for the theater?

Fairy tales gathered other secularized myths, adventure stories, legends, and anecdotes around the primitive magical core. In addition to the magical characters, the characters of the peasant world became stock characters. (For example, the clever hero and the simpleton.) A dense and complex magma was created; a skein of a hundred colors whose most important thread, according to Propp, is the immediate description of events.

One theory can be just as valid as the next, and perhaps none is able to deliver a complete explanation of the fairy tale. Propp's theory is particularly fascinating because it establishes a profound connection between the prehistorical boy, who experienced the rituals, and the historical boy, who is introduced into the human world with the fairy tale as part of his initiation—many would say on the level of the collective unconscious. The identification that the little listener makes with Little Tom Thumb from the fairy tale, told to the boy by his mother, does not only have a psychological justification in light of this theory, but also a much more profound one, rooted in the obscurity of blood.

Analyzing the structure of the folk tale—paying particular attention to the Russian folk tale (which largely belongs to the same Indo-European heritage as the German or Italian folk tales)—Propp succeeded in formulating three principles: 1) "Functions of characters serve as stable, constant elements in a tale, independent of how and by whom they are fulfilled. They constitute the fundamental components of a tale." 2) "The number of the functions known to the fairy tale is limited." 3) "The sequence of functions is always identical."

In Propp's system there are thirty-one functions, and they are sufficient, along with their variants and internal articulations, to describe the form of the fairy tale:

1) absentation (One of the members of a family absents himself from home.)

2) interdiction (An interdiction is addressed to the hero.)

3) violation (The interdiction is violated.)

4) reconnaissance (The villain makes an attempt at reconnaissance.)

5) delivery (The villain receives information about his victim.)

6) trickery (The villain attempts to deceive his victim.)

7) complicity (The victim submits to deception and thereby unwittingly helps his enemy.)

8) villainy (The villain causes harm or injury to a member of a family.)

9) mediation (The misfortune or lack becomes known.)

10) beginning counteraction (The seeker agrees to or decides upon a counteraction.)

11) departure (The hero leaves home.)

12) the first function of the donor (The hero is tested, preparing the way for magical help.)

13) the hero's reaction (The hero reacts to the actions of the future donor.)

14) provision of a magical agent (The hero acquires the use of a magical agent.)

15) spatial transference between two kingdoms (The hero is led to the object of his search.)

16) struggle (The hero and the villain join in direct combat.)

17) branding, marking (The hero is branded.)

18) victory (The villain is defeated.)

19) removal of misfortune (The initial lack is liquidated.)

20) return (The hero returns.)

21) pursuit, chase (The hero is pursued.)

22) rescue (Rescue of the hero from pursuit.)

23) unrecognized arrival (The hero, unrecognized, arrives home or in another country.)

24) unfounded claims (A false hero presents unfounded claims.)

25) difficult task (A difficult task is proposed to the hero.)

26) fulfillment (The task is fulfilled.)

27) recognition (The hero is recognized.)

28) exposure (The false hero or villain is exposed.)

29) transfiguration (The hero is given a new appearance.)

30) punishment (The villain is punished.)

31) wedding (The hero is married and ascends the throne.)

Naturally not *all* these functions can be found in all fairy tales. In the obligatory sequence there are jumps, additions, and syntheses that do not, however, contradict the general line of action. A fairy tale can begin with the first function, the seventh, or the twelfth, but—if it is an old one—it is difficult to jump backward to recuperate passages that have been left out.

The function of absentation, which Propp places in the first position, can be performed by a character who leaves home for some reason, a prince who departs for war, a father who dies, a parent who goes off to work (telling the children—here we have the interdiction or prohibition—not to open the door to anyone, or not to touch a particular thing), a merchant who begins a business trip, et cetera. Each function can include its opposite: the interdiction can be represented by a positive command.

But I want to move on with my observations about Propp's functions to suggest to those readers who would like to experiment with this scheme that they test the sequences with any one of the films about James Bond. Whoever tries this experiment will be surprised to find how many functions there are in such a film and in almost the same sequence. Here we can see how alive and persistently present the fairy tale structure is in our culture. Many adventure books follow the same sequence.

The functions are interesting because we can use them to construct an infinite number of stories, just as one can compose any number of melodies with twelve notes (omitting the quarter tones and always staying within the limited musical system of the West before the rise of electronic music).

In Reggio Emilia we wanted to see how productive Propp's functions could be. We experimented with a group of children, choosing twenty functions, skipping some and substituting others while indicating how they corresponded to other fairy tale motifs. Two painter friends of mine created twenty "playing cards," and each card was marked with a word (the "title" of the function) and illustrated with a pertinent symbol or caricature: "prohibition," "violation," "damage or lack," "departure of the hero," "task," "meeting with the donor," "magical gifts," "the appearance of the villain," "demonic powers of the villain," "combat," "victory," "return," "arrival at home," "the false hero," "difficult tasks," "fulfillment of the tasks," "recognition of the hero," "the false hero exposed," "punishment of the antagonist," and "marriage."

The children worked together and produced a story, structuring it according to the series of the twenty "cards of Propp." All this was done with a great deal of leeway, it must be said, and with the most remarkable results of parody.

I saw how easily children succeed in producing a fairy tale following the sequence of the cards because each word of the series (each function or fairy tale motif), as far as the fairy tale is concerned, is full of meaning and also lends itself to a game with an infinite number of variations. I remember a very original interpretation of "interdiction": a father leaves the house and tells his children not to throw flower vases from the balcony onto the heads of pedestrians. . . . And among the "difficult tasks," there is the command to go to the cemetery at midnight. Up to a certain age, this task acquires a maximum of terror and requires a maximum of courage.

Children love to mix the cards and to improvise and change the rules: draw three cards at random and form a complete story; take off from the last card of the series; divide the cards between two groups that are having a contest to invent the most original story. Frequently, one card is sufficient to suggest an entire fairy tale. The card with the title "magic gifts" was enough to prompt a fourth grader to invent a story about a pen that did homework assignments by itself.

Anyone can make a pack of "cards of Propp" with twenty or thirty pieces of paper, or fifty, depending on what one wants to do. It is enough to write the title of the function or the motif on each card. Illustrations are not required.

This game can erroneously recall the structure of the "puzzle" or the "riddle," in which twenty to a thousand fragments are present, and the tasks consist in reconstructing the entire design in mosaic fashion. In contrast, the "cards of Propp" allow, as I noted, for the construction of an infinite number of pictures because each piece does not have a unique meaning, but is open to many meanings.

Why should one use just the "cards of Propp" and not some other cards of fantasy, or a group of pictures taken at random, or a series of words from a dictionary? It seems evident to me: each "card of Propp" represents not merely itself, but an entire section of the fairy tale world, a swarm of fantastic echoes, for children who have become familiar with the fairy tales, their language, and their motifs.

Moreover, each function is rich in appeals to the personal world of the child. Indeed, a child reads "prohibition" or "interdiction," and the word enters into immediate contact with the experience that he or she has had with familiar prohibitions ("don't touch," "don't play in the water," "don't pick up the hammer"). The child relives obscurely the first moments of his or her relationship to things, when only the "yes" and the "no" of the mother helped distinguish between what was allowed and what was forbidden. For the child, "prohibited" is the confrontation with the authority or authoritarian rule of the school. But there is also a positive sense ("prohibition" and "order" are functionally equivalent) when it leads to the discovery of the rules of the game: "This is the way to do it, not that way." The encounter with the limits that reality or society imposes on the child's liberty is one of the instruments of the child's socialization.

The structure of the fairy tale is not only a recasting of the rites of initiation—if we agree with Propp—but it also mirrors in some way the structure of the child's experience, which is a series of missions and duels, of difficult tests and disappointments, representing certain inevitable stages of life. This includes even the experience of "magical gifts"—those of Santa Claus and the Easter Bunny. Parents remain the "magical donors" for a long time, capable of everything. Children populate their universe with powerful allies and diabolical enemies for a long time. It seems to me that in some way the fairy tale functions help children shed light on their own lives. And the functions are there, ready, fully tested, easy to use. In my opinion, to discard them would be squandering a good opportunity.

Though this chapter has become too long, I would still like to add two more observations.

The first regards a point that Propp made while studying the Russian folk tale and the transformation of a particular motif. He took the motif of the "hut on chicken feet in the forest" and traced all its concrete variants during its development: through *reduction* (the little hut on chicken feet; the hut in the forest; the hut; the forest); through *amplification* (the little hut in the forest with cinnamon walls and a gingerbread roof); through *substitution* (instead of the hut, there is a grotto or a castle); through *intensification* (an entire magical realm). Here we can note how Propp makes use of almost the same terms in which Saint Augustine describes the work of the imagination that consists of "setting up, multiplying, reducing, extending, ordering, recomposing images in any way whatsoever."

The second observation is based on something that I remember. In the home of Antonio Faeti (both a painter and a teacher and also author of the unusual book, *Guardare le figure* [*Looking at Faces*]), I saw a series of great pictures based on the functions of Propp. Each of them was a story that developed on different levels. The hero was not only a child with his fantasies, his complexes, and his deep unconsciousness, but also a man and his adventures, and also the painter and his culture. His dense paintings were populated with images, allusions, and citations that stretched out their tentacles to the popular broadside as well as to surrealism. They were "cards of Propp" by an artist who loves an extraordinarily rich world in fairy tales, a world that is foolishly marginalized. Each painting says an enormous amount that could be expressed by words, but only by a few words. Others say a great deal that cannot be expressed by words.

20 • Changing the Cards into a Fairy Tale with Franco Passatore

IN THE PREVIOUS CHAPTER, when I wrote about preserving the presence of the folk tale in the games of invention, I did not mean to insist that its presence be obligatory. Along with the "cards of Propp," there can be other entertaining games that are no less productive.

I would like to cite as example the wonderful game invented by Franco Passatore and his friends in the Gruppo Teatro-Gioco-Vita (The Theater-Play-Life Group). This game is called "Let's change the cards into a fairy tale." It is described in the book *Io ero l'albero (tu il cavallo)* (*I Was the Tree, You the Horse*) by Franco Passatore, Silvio De Stefanis, Ave Fontana, and Flavia De Lucis, in the chapter "Quaranta e piú giochi per vivere la scuola," ("Forty and More Games to Experience School"):

> The game consists of inventing and illustrating a collective story. It can be stimulated by a suitable pack of cards prepared by the animator or facilitator. Figures and pictures cut out of newspapers and magazines are pasted on approximately fifty large cards. The reading of these images is always different because each card of the pack is connected to the preceding one only by the free association of ideas or, at least, by the play of imagination. The animator is seated in the middle of a circle of children and asks one of them to choose a card at random. The child must interpret it verbally, thereby providing the

beginning of a collective story. The child's exposition is the basis for his or her illustration on white cardstock or a roll of paper—it can be a drawing or a collage—and this is the first part of the story. The next student continues the story by picking another card. He or she interprets it by illustrating the narrative development with a drawing or a collage connected to the preceding one. The game continues this way until the last child has a chance, and he or she must bring the story to an end. The result is a long illustrated panel by all the children on which they can visually re-read their collective story.

In the book, the game was presented with the title *spettacolazione*, a little play that had not yet been performed. By this time, I hope, hundreds of children have "changed the cards into a fairy tale" and have presented the animators of these games with a sufficient amount of material for reflection.

This game seems wonderful to me. It is so wonderful that I wish I had invented it myself. But I am not jealous of Franco Passatore and his friends. I have seen them work in Rome during a festival organized by the newspaper *L'Unità*. They know a great number of inventive games and have techniques to excite children that have been tried and tested in dozens of experiments. For example, they give children three different objects—a coffee can, an empty bottle, and a hoe—and then invite the children to invent and act out a scene with these objects. It is almost like inventing a story with three words, but it is much better, evidently, because the objects offer the imagination a much more solid prop than the words: they can be watched, touched, and handled, and numerous fantastic ideas can be drawn from them. The story can spring from a casual gesture, from a noise. . . . Moreover, the collective character of the invention is bound to have a stimulating effect: diverse experiences, personal memories and rhythms, and the critical function of the group enter into play and are compared with one another in a creative way.

The Gruppo Teatro-Gioco-Vita believes in objects. Frequently, when they want to stimulate the children to draw, they give each child a mysterious box in which there is a ball of cotton that smells like gas, a piece of candy, or something that smells like chocolate. Inspiration can also be stimulated by smells.

In the games of the Gruppo the children are simultaneously the authors, actors, and spectators of all that happens. The situation stimulates their creativity at all times and in many different directions.

21 • Fairy Tales in the "Obligatory Key"

IN PAYING HOMAGE to the game of transforming the cards into a fairy tale, we had put aside oral folk tales for a moment. Now I want to return to them to demonstrate one last technical application. Perhaps I should have talked about this before dealing with the "functions" of Propp. Then my explication would have been more regular. But it has almost become strictly required nowadays to introduce some irregularities into a grammar. So, the technique that I shall now discuss can be wonderfully applied to all the "cards of Propp," and the cards themselves contribute to making the technique more clear.

As I have shown, within each fairy tale "function" there is an infinite number of variations possible. The technique of each variation, however, can be applied to the entire fairy tale, which in turn can be modulated and transposed from one conceivable musical register to another.

The fantastic theme can be: "Tell the story of the Pied Piper of Hamlin but make it take place in Rome of 1973."

The introduction of this key (or, if you will, two keys—of time and place) obligates us to search for the point in the old tale where we can begin the modulation. It is actually possible to imagine the Rome of 1973 invaded by rats without falling into the absurd. But it would probably not be very productive. Rome is indeed invaded, not by rats, but by cars that block the streets, swamp all the squares and small parks, cover the sidewalks and rob space from the pedestrians, and prevent children from playing on them. Thus we have a fantastic hypothesis at our disposal that incorporates a large chunk of reality into the frame of the fairy tale, and it is the best that we can hope for. Here is a part of the composition in the new key:

> Rome is invaded by cars—and here it would be a useful exercise to describe the invasion using fairy tale terms, with parking places on the top of Saint Peter's Cathedral, but we do not have time for this. The mayor offers a reward and his own daughter in marriage to any man who can get rid of the cars. A young musician appears, similar to one of those who circulate in Rome during Christmas time and play bagpipes. He says he will free metropolitan Rome of cars if in turn the mayor promises that the majority of public places will be reserved for children so they can play there. The mayor agrees. The musician begins playing his song, and the cars start following him from every corner, niche, district, and suburb. Meanwhile he heads toward the Tiber. The owners of the cars are in semi-revolt. (In the final analysis, the cars are the fruit of human labor, and to destroy them is a bad thing.) They manage to convince

the musician, and he changes direction and takes a road that leads underground. The cars can continue to be driven and parked, but beneath the ground. Consequently the streets and places above ground are left to the children, the bank clerks, the fruit dealers, et cetera.

In the chapter about "Recasting Fairy Tales," we already conceived of a Cinderella in an "interplanetary key" and a Hansel and Gretel in a "Milanese key." There appear to be no limits to the invention of new "keys." In reality they can all be grasped, that is, almost all, under the category time and space.

The old fairy tale, tuned in the new key, adapts itself to the new performance, brings forth unexpected sounds. It can even have a moral—that we accept, if it is organic and authentic—but we do not have to impose one arbitrarily.

In a middle school, where the students were required to follow the traditional bureaucratic approach to Manzoni's *I promessi sposi* (*The Betrothed*)—recapitulation of the story, analysis of grammar, questions, themes—the students listened with very little enthusiasm to my proposal to create a new version of the novel in modern dress. However, after they discovered the possibilities of the game by improvising and recognizing parallels between Manzoni's peasants of the nineteenth century and the Italian fascists and German Nazis of the 1930s and 1940s, the students threw themselves into it in a serious way.

According to the new key, Lucia continued to be a worker in a textile mill of Lombardy. But the chosen period of time—1944, during the Nazi occupation—compelled Renzo, a major protagonist, to join the underground resistance to avoid being sent to a forced labor camp in Germany. The plague was represented by the Allied bombings of Italy. The boss of the district, who held all the power and kept bothering Lucia, was none other than the local commander of the fascist "Black Brigade." Don Abbondio was always himself, eternally torn between the partisans and the fascists, the workers and the bosses, and the Italians and the foreigners. The unidentified man behind the scenes was a great industrialist from this region, formerly a supporter of the regime, who provided a safe place for refugees and war victims in his villa during the occupation.

I don't think that Alessandro Manzoni, if he had by chance been present, would have had any reason to be offended by the use that the students made of his characters. Perhaps Manzoni would have helped them to understand and to develop certain analogies. And he alone would have been able to suggest to Don Abbondio some witty remarks to fit the new situation.

22 • The Analysis of La Befana

IF WE BREAK DOWN the fairy tale into "prime factors" with the purpose of discovering the elements to construct new fantastic binominals, we can call this process the "fantastic analysis" of a fairy tale character, and it can also help us invent other stories using this character.

Let us take La Befana, known in Italian folklore as the good witch who, like Santa Claus, delivers gifts (she does so on the night of the Epiphany). She is really not common in fairy tales, but she will do anyway. If we use her in this exercise instead of a normal fairy tale witch, we can demonstrate that this analysis can be applied to any kind of character, from Little Tom Thumb to Ulysses, from Pinocchio to Buffalo Bill.

With respect to Propp's functions, we can define La Befana as a "donor." In the analysis, La Befana is divided into three parts, just as Caesar divided Gaul, and Dante *The Divine Comedy*:

1) her broom
2) her sack filled with presents
3) her worn-out shoes

Certainly, La Befana can be divided differently, and one can do as one pleases. But, for my purposes, this division into three is sufficient.

Each one of the three prime factors can furnish a creative spark, provided that we know methodically how to investigate the possibilities to ignite it.

1) *The broom.* Usually La Befana uses it for flying. But if we take the object out of its usual context, we may ask: What does La Befana do with it after Twelfth-night? This question, in turn, engenders numerous hypotheses:

a) At the end of her trip around the earth, La Befana flies to other worlds of the solar system and of the galaxy.

b) La Befana uses the broom to clean her house. Where does she live? What does she do the entire year? Does she get mail? Does she like coffee? Does she read the newspaper?

c) There is not only one Befana, there are many. They live in the country of Befanas where the most important business is understandably the manufacture of brooms. There is the Befana of Reggio Emilia, the Befana of Omegna, and the Befana of Rome, who all use the brooms. The consumption of brooms is remarkable. A Befana who is smart can increase her business by continually launching a new fashion: one year it is the mini-broom; the year after, the maxi-broom; then the midi-broom, et cetera. A Befana gets rich and begins a business of vacuum cleaners. Now the Befanas travel with that appliance, causing considerable cosmic confusion. The vacuum cleaner sucks in the dust of the stars, captures birds, comets, an airplane with all the passengers (who are then deposited at home through the chimney, or, if there is no chimney, on the kitchen terrace).

2) *The sack filled with presents.* The hypothesis that occurs to me right away is that the sack has a hole in it. I shall pursue this hypothesis without asking myself why, so that I do not waste any time:

a) While La Befana is flying, the presents slip through the hole and fall to the earth. A doll lands near the den of some wolves, who are fooled. "Ah," says the wolf, "it's like the time of Romulus and Remus. Fame is within easy reach." They bring up the doll with love, but it does not grow. The wolf cubs play, with no thought of fame. But if we choose to have it grow, the doll can have an exciting destiny in the forest—it will be a Tarzan doll, a Queen of Sheba doll. . . .

b) A list of gifts and a list of recipients are prepared. The individual gifts and the individual recipients are matched by chance. (The hole in the sack is, in reality, an opening toward chance, not necessarily an opening toward chaos.) A mink coat—a gift ordered by a prestigious senator for his girlfriend—lands in Sardinia at the feet of a shepherd watching over his sheep during a cold winter's night. Well done. . . .

c) Let us sew up the hole in the sack, and let us once again assume that there are many Befanas. Therefore, there are many sacks. If each Befana makes a mistake and becomes confused when they all depart, the Befana of Reggio Emilia will carry her toys to Domodossola, the Befana of Massalombarda will carry hers to Minervino Murge. When they realize their mistakes, the Befanas are upset. They take a trip to check all the damage that they have caused. But there is no damage: throughout the world the children are the same and love the same toys. (But the conclusion to be drawn from this is not necessarily poetical: throughout the world the children are accustomed to the same toys because the same large corporations manufacture them. The children all choose the same things because they have already been chosen for them.)

3) *The worn-out shoes.* As fantastic objects, the worn-out shoes—generally neglected in the analyses—are just as productive as the broom and the gifts.

a) La Befana decides to procure a pair of new shoes, and in each house she visits to bring gifts, she searches for shoes. Finally she finishes by stealing a pair of shoes owned by a poor retired teacher who owns only one pair of shoes.

b) The children learn that La Befana has worn-out shoes, and they feel sorry for her. They write letters to newspapers. A TV station begins collecting donations for her. A band of swindlers goes from house to house gathering the donations and makes off with the money. Altogether they collect a hundred thousand dollars, and they spend the money in Switzerland and Singapore.

c) On the night of January 6, the night when La Befana traditionally distributes gifts, the compassionate children place a pair of new shoes for her next to the stocking hung up to receive gifts. The Befana of Vigevano sees the shoes before the other Befanas. She goes from house to house before the others and collects two hundred thousand pairs of shoes. (Yes, there are two hundred thousand children with good hearts.) Once she returns to her area, she opens up a large shoe store and becomes rich. Afterwards, she, too, goes to Switzerland and Singapore.

I do not claim to have made a complete analysis of La Befana with the examination above. I have simply tried to show how the fantastic analysis can enable the imagination to work with simple data: a word, a meeting, or a clash between two words or between a fairy tale element and a real one. That is, this kind of analysis offers us elementary oppositions in which the imagination articulates its story, sets off fantastical hypotheses, and allows the introduction of "keys" (for example the "spatial key"). In sum, we are dealing here with an exercise in which numerous techniques of invention intervene at the same time, bringing about "the analysis of analysis." But that would be a bit too much pedantry, wouldn't it?

23 · The Little Glass Man

IF THERE IS a given character, a real one (like La Befana or Little Tom Thumb)—or an imaginary one (like the little glass man, this is the first that comes to my mind)—his or her adventures can be logically deduced from his characteristics. But what does "logically" mean here? Is it related to a *fantastical logic* or a *logical logic*? I wouldn't know. Perhaps it is both.

For this reason let us take the glass man. He must act, move, interrelate with his surroundings, experience mishaps, and cause events because of the nature of the material out of which we have conceived him.

The analysis of this material will enable us to see the laws of this character:

Glass is transparent. The glass man is transparent. The thoughts in his head can be read. He does not need to speak to communicate. He cannot tell lies because they would be immediately seen unless he wore a hat. It would be a bad day in the country of glass men when it became fashionable to wear hats—that is, fashionable to conceal one's thoughts.

Glass is fragile. The house of the glass man would have to be completely cushioned. The sidewalks are covered with mattresses. It is forbidden to shake hands! Hard labor is forbidden. The true doctor of the country is the glazier.

Glass can be colored. It is washable, et cetera. In my encyclopedia, there are four large pages dedicated to glass, and almost every line contains a word whose meaning could be used in the story about glass men. It is all printed there in black and white, next to all sorts of information related to chemistry, physics, industry, commodity production, and who knows what else. But its place in a fairy tale is ensured.

The character made of wood must watch out for fire that can burn its feet. It can easily float in water. Its fist is as hard as a stick. If it is hanged, it does not die. The fish cannot eat it. All of these things are exactly what happens to Pinocchio because he is made out of wood. If Pinocchio were made out of steel, he would have entirely different kinds of adventures.

A man made of ice, ice cream, or butter can live only in a refrigerator. Otherwise he would melt. His adventures take place between the freezer and the fresh salad.

A man made out of carbon paper will have completely different adventures from the man made of marble, straw, chocolate, plastic, smoke, or marzipan.

In this domain, the analysis of commodity logic and the fantastic analysis coincide almost perfectly. It is not up to me to say that it is better to make windows with glass and Easter eggs with chocolate, but rather the fairy tale: it is particularly in this type of story that the imagination plays between the real and the imaginary in a see-saw manner that remains highly instructive, even indispensable, for mastering the real in depth, for reshaping it.

24 • Piano Jack

THE CHARACTERS of comic books are not different from our glass men or straw men. Each one follows the logic of the attribute that distinguishes it from others and that is sufficient to make it continually encounter new adventures—or always the same adventure, repeated in infinite variations and modifications. In this case, the attribute is not physical, but is of another nature, generally moral.

If we take the characteristics of Scrooge McDuck—very rich, stingy, and boastful—and if we take the characteristics of his friends and antagonists, anyone can easily imagine a hundred thousand stories. The true and proper invention of these "periodical" characters takes place one single time. The rest is, in the best cases, variation; in the worst, formula and exploitation in the extreme, the production of serials.

After the children have read a dozen or a hundred stories about Scrooge McDuck—an exercise that is nevertheless fun—they are perfectly capable of inventing their own by themselves. Once they have fulfilled their duty as consumers, they should be placed in a position to act as creators. It is a shame that very few people think about this.

To invent and draw a comic book is, after all is said and done, much more fulfilling than to write a theme about Mother's Day or some "noble" president. The comic book affords children the opportunity to create the idea of a story, its "treatment," its design and organization in individual scenes; to invent dialogue, the physical and moral characterization of its figures, et cetera. These are all things that children sometimes do alone to amuse themselves, if they are intelligent. And in the meantime they receive an F in Italian or English at school.

Sometimes the principal attribute of a character can be personified by an object, such as Popeye and his can of spinach.

Let us invent a pair of twins by the name of Marco and Mirco who always run about armed with hammers. The twins can be told apart only by their hammers: Marco's hammer has a white handle; Mirco's, a black one. Their adventures are already predictable, whether they encounter a thief, or whether they come upon a ghost, vampire, or werewolf. It can be deduced from the hammers that they will always triumph. They were born without fear and inhibition. They are aggressive and ready to fight to the bitter end against all sorts of monsters (but certainly with many misunderstandings).

Attention: I wrote "hammers," not "clubs." These characters have nothing at all in common with two little neo-fascists.

The strong ideological content of this invention—please allow me this digression—should not be misleading. It has not been programmed but has arisen by itself. I once thought of writing something about the twins of my friend Arturo, who named them Marco and Amerigo. I wrote their names on a piece of paper, and without realizing it I rewrote and changed them into principal characters of this exercise. That is how I got the names

Marco and Mirko, which are more symmetrical, more twin-like than the original names. The word hammer (*martello*)—which arrived third—was evidently a result of the syllable *mar* from Marco, partly contradicted but also partly reinforced by *mir* from Mirco. In the plural, hammers (*martelli*) arose more out of a sense of rhyme from twins (*gemelli*) and hammers (*martelli*), than out of a logical consideration. This was not explicit but implicit. This is how I came to the image of the two twins armed with hammers. The rest was deduction.

There are also characters whose names simply "tell" everything about them. Such are the "pirate," the "bandit," the "pioneer," the "Indian," the "cowboy," et cetera.

If we would like to invent a new cowboy, we would have to choose his attribute with great care. Or his peculiar mannerism. Or an object that is most emblematic of him.

A courageous cowboy? That is banal. A bronco buster has been used too often. A cowboy who plays the guitar or banjo is traditional. Let us vary the instruments. A cowboy who plays the piano is more promising. . . . But perhaps it would be better if he carries it with him on a pack horse.

Is his name Piano Jack or Billy the Piano Player? He always travels with two horses; he is on the first, and the piano is on the second. He rides alone through the Rocky Mountains. Whenever he sets up camp, he sets the piano on the ground and plays a Brahms lullaby or Beethoven's variations of a waltz by Diabelli. The wolves and the wild boars come from afar to hear him. The cows, in love with the music, give more milk. In the inevitable encounters with bandits or sheriffs, Piano Jack does not need pistols. He scares away his enemies by playing some Bach fugues, atonal dissonances, excerpts from Bela Bartók's *Microcosmos*. Et cetera.

25 • Eating and "Play-Eating"

"THE DEVELOPMENT of the mental processes," wrote L. S. Vygotsky in *Thought and Language*, "is initiated by a dialogue from the words and gestures between the child and the parents. Autonomous thinking begins when the child is first capable of internalizing these conversations and instituting them within himself or herself."

After having discarded many other quotations, I chose this one to begin a brief series of observations about the "household imagination," which takes its impetus from maternal discourse, because it seems to me that

Vygotsky has said in a clear and simple manner what others struggle to articulate.

The dialogue the Soviet psychologist discusses is first of all a monologue, maternal or paternal, made of tender sounds, of encouragements and smiles, of small events. From time to time these events spark recognition and surprise. They cause the global response of toddling and the prelinguistic music of stammering. Above all, from the very first weeks of the child's life, a mother never tires of talking to her infant as if she wanted to keep the baby in a womb of tender and warm words. She acts spontaneously, as if she had read what Maria Montessori says about the "absorbing mind" of the child that to a certain degree internalizes the language and all kinds of signals from the outside world through "absorption."

"He doesn't understand, but he is contented. So something is happening," remarks a mother to a pediatrician who is very rational. This mother talks to her child in the crib as she would to an adult. "Somehow he listens to me."

"He doesn't listen to you, he watches you. He's contented because you're there and you're taking care of him."

"He understands something, and something happens," responds the mother.

Even to associate a voice with a face is work; it is the fruit of an elementary mental activity. By speaking to a child who is not yet able to understand her, the mother still does a useful thing not only because she offers him her company, her protection and warmth, but also because she nourishes his hunger for stimuli.

The maternal discourse is often imaginative and poetical, causing the bathing and feeding rituals and the change of diapers to be transformed into a game for two, accompanied by inventive gestures.

"I'm certain that he laughs when I put his little shoes on his hands instead of on his feet."

A six-month-old child amused himself a great deal when his mother pretended to stick a spoonful of food in her ear while feeding him. With great joy and excitement, he demanded the repetition of this scene.

Some of these games have been institutionalized within our Western tradition. For example, when feeding cereal to an infant, it is most common to encourage the child to take another spoonful for the aunt, the grandmother, et cetera. But this custom is not completely reasonable, as I think I can demonstrate with the following ditty:

A spoonful for mama,
A spoonful for papa,

A spoonful for grandma
Down in Alabama,
A spoonful for auntie
Who lives in Miami.
Oh, poor little baby
With aches in your belly.

But the child takes part freely in this game, at least to a certain age, because it catches his attention, populates his meal with people so that it becomes almost like a "royal *déjeuner*." Indeed, the game gives a symbolical significance to the act of eating and frees it from the routine of daily monotony and obligation. Eating becomes an aesthetic fact, a playing at eating, a meal recital. Likewise, the act of getting dressed and undressed becomes more interesting when it takes the form of "playing at getting dressed and undressed." Here I would like to ask Franco Passatore whether or not these games would fit his definition of "theater-play-life," but I don't have his telephone number.

The more patient mothers have the means to ascertain daily the value of "playing at. . . ." One mother told me that her child had learned very quickly how to button her clothes by herself because she repeatedly told her child the story about "Little Button" while buttoning her child's clothes. This story is about a little button who searches for its little house and keeps going into the wrong house, but then it is extremely happy when it finally succeeds in slipping into its own home. Of course, this mother also used the word "little door," contributing to a certain condescending use of the diminutive that should be avoided whenever possible. But the process is wonderful and significant and says a great deal about the importance of the imagination in educating children.

It would be wrong to believe, however, that the story of the button would keep its fascination if written down and published. It is part of a precious "family lexicon," if I may borrow this term from Natalia Ginzburg. It would no longer have any sense for the child if she were to find it again in a book, after she has known for some time how to button her clothes by herself, and when she is beginning to ask for more substantial adventures from printed books.

It seems to me that a closer analysis of the "maternal discourse" is indispensable for those who want to invent stories for the tiniest children, even tinier than Little Tom Thumb.

26 • Stories at the Table

THE MOTHER who pretended to put a spoonful of food into her ear used one of the essential principles of artistic creation without knowing it. She "estranged" the spoon from the world of banality and thus gave it a new meaning or attribute. Children do the same thing when they use a chair to make a train, or transform a toy car in the bathtub into a ship, or assign a teddy bear the role of an airplane. This was exactly what Hans Christian Andersen did when he turned a needle and a thimble into characters who experienced certain adventures.

Stories for the smallest children can be invented by animating the objects that can be found at the table or on the high chair when it is time to eat. And if I add some examples here it is not because I want to teach mothers how to be mothers, God help me, but because one should never assert anything without providing a demonstration. This is why I offer the following few examples for analysis:

The spoon. The mother's "incorrect" gesture gives rise to others. The spoon does not know where to go. It heads for the eye. It attacks the nose and presents us with a binominal spoon-nose, that would be a shame to waste. "Once upon a time there was a man with a spoon-nose. He could not eat soup because his spoon-nose could never find his mouth. . . ."

If we play with the binominal and vary the second term, we come up with water-faucet-nose, pipe-nose, lamp-nose. . . .

"A man had a water faucet as a nose. It was very comfortable. Instead of blowing his nose, he opened and closed the faucet. One day the faucet started to drip. . . ." (In this story, the child re-encounters some of his own experiences and can laugh about them. The relation that one has to one's own nose is not always easy.)

"A man had a pipe-nose. He was a heavy smoker. . . . There was once a nose-lamp. It turned itself on and off. It provided light at the table. Whenever it sneezed, it blew a bulb, and one had to change it. . . ."

After the spoon gives rise to these stories about the nose that obviously have interesting psychoanalytical backgrounds (and that is why they can touch the child more directly than we think), it can become an autonomous character. It walks, runs, and jumps. It has amorous adventures with a fork. Its rival is a terrible knife. In this new situation the fairy tale assumes a double aspect: on the one hand it follows, or provokes, the real movements of the spoon as object; on the other hand, it creates a Mr. Spoon in whom the object is reduced to a mere name with its one virtue of evocation. "Mr. Spoon was very tall, exceedingly thin, and had a large head that was so heavy he could not stand on his feet. It was more comfortable for him to walk on his head. Thus he saw the whole world upside down, and his ideas were always mistaken. . . ." The animation of an object leads to personification, as in the tales by Andersen.

The saucer. If the child is left alone, he or she will spontaneously invent a symbolical use, such as transforming an object into a car or airplane. Why should we forbid a child to do this? So what if every now and then the child breaks a saucer? It is better if we, who know more, would consider intensifying the game.

The saucer flies. It flies to grandmother, to the aunt, to the father in the factory. . . . What should it say to them? What will they say to it? We stand up, accompany the "flight" (with the hand) of the plate across the room while it approaches a window, flies through a door, disappears, and returns with some candy or with a little surprise to be unwrapped.

The saucer is an airplane. The spoon is the pilot. It flies around the lamp as if it were flying around the sun. It takes a trip around the world. It's enough simply to provide the word. . . .

The saucer is a turtle. . . . It is a snail. The cup is its house. (However, I'll leave the cup for readers to use for their exercises.)

The sugar. If we break down the sugar into its primary elements—it is white, sweet, and like sand. It offers us three ways of invention—according to its color, taste, and form. While I was writing "sweet," I suddenly thought what would happen if there were no more sugar in the world. All the sweet things would immediately become bitter. The grandmother would want to drink her coffee, but it would be so bitter that she'd assume that she had put salt in it instead of sugar. A bitter world. It is all the fault of an evil magician. A bitter magician. (I am offering this character to the first person who raises his or her hand.)

The disappearance of the sugar permits me to insert here—and I do this without parentheses to give it the right emphasis—a hint about a process that I shall call the "fantastic subtraction." It consists in making all the objects of this world disappear one after the other. *The sun disappears.* It no longer shines. The world is always dark. . . . *The money disappears.* The stock market is in chaos. . . . *The paper disappears.* All the vegetables packed in paper begin rolling on the ground. . . . Object after object is subtracted until we arrive at a completely empty world, a world of nothing. . . .

> Once upon a time there was a little man made of nothing. He walked down a street of nothing that went nowhere. He met a cat made of nothing that had whiskers of nothing, a tail of nothing, claws of nothing. . . .

I already wrote this story. Is it useful? I believe so. Children play "the game of nothing" themselves, when they close their eyes. It enables them to give shape to things and to separate appearance from their existence. The table becomes extraordinarily important right at that moment in which, while I look at it, I say, "the table no longer exists." It is as if I were to look at it for the first time, not to see how it is made—I know that—but to perceive that it is, that it exists.

I am convinced that children begin to intuit this relationship between being and not being very early. Sometimes you can surprise children as they let their eyelids sink in order to let the things disappear, and then they raise them in order to see them reappear. They repeat this process patiently. The philosopher who investigates the question of Being and Nothingness, using the capital letters that these respectable and profound concepts deserve, does not do anything substantially different than continue that children's game at a higher level.

27 • A Journey around My House

WHAT IS A TABLE for a one-year-old child apart from the use that adults make of it? It is a roof. The child can squat beneath it and feel like the master of the house—of a house made to measure not so large and terrible as the house of the grown-ups. A chair is interesting because it can be shoved back and forth and one can measure one's own strength by doing this. The chair can be turned over and dragged, and a child can climb on top of it. The chair can be beaten if it maliciously hits you on the head: "Naughty chair!"

For us, the table and the chair are consummate objects and almost invisible. We use them automatically, but children regard them as materials of an ambivalent and multi-dimensional nature to be explored for a long time. Here, cognition and narration, experience and symbolization, work hand in hand. While children learn to become familiar with the surface of these things, they do not stop playing with them. Nor do they stop formulating hypotheses about their value and making imaginative use of their positive elements that they themselves have conceived. Thus, they learn that when you open a faucet, water will run out, and this notion forms part of their knowledge. But this does not prevent them from believing, provided that this is the case, that "from the other side" there is a "man" who pours water into the pipe so that it can come out of the faucet.

The child does not know the "principle of contradiction." The child is a scientist, but also an "animist" ("naughty chair!") and "artificialist" ("there is a man who pours water into the pipe"). These characters live together in the child for a good number of years in varying degrees.

A question arises from the evidence: Are we doing a good thing by telling children stories in which the protagonists are household objects, or do we risk encouraging them in their animism and artificialism at the cost of their scientific spirit?

I ask this question more from scruple than concern. Playing with things enables one to get to know them better. And I do not see any use in limiting the freedom of play because that would be like negating the formative and cognitive function of play. The imagination is not a "bad wolf" to be feared, or a criminal who must be constantly persecuted and carefully controlled. It is up to me, from time to time, to understand whether or not the child at a given moment desires "information about the faucet" or wants "to play with the faucet" in order to obtain information to be used in his or her way.

This premise has enabled me to deduce some useful principles for enriching the dialogue with children about household objects:

1) To begin, I must take into account that the first adventure of the child, as soon as he or she is able to get down from the high chair or to get out of the prison of the "playpen," is the discovery of the house, the furniture and machines that populate it, their forms and their uses. They provide children with the material of their first observations and feelings that they will use to form a vocabulary that functions as indices of the world in which they are growing. Within the limits that the child sets and tolerates, I shall tell him or her "true stories" about things, without forgetting that— to a great extent—these "true stories" will sound to the child like a mere verbal chain, a point where the imagination can apply itself, neither more nor less than the fairy tale. If I say where water comes from, words like *source, basin, pipe, river, lake,* et cetera remain suspended in the child during the search for an object until the child has seen and touched the thing indicated. It would already be better if I had a complete series of illustrated albums at my disposal such as "Where does water come from?" "Where does the table come from?" "Where does the glass for windows come from?" and other similar books that would at least demonstrate the forms of things. But such albums do not always exist. A "literature" for children from zero to three has not yet been studied systematically or produced. It has only come about through sporadic intuition.

2) I associate the child's animism and artificialism with the sources of invention without fear of introducing or reinforcing "mistaken" explanations. On the contrary, I think that in some way the "animistic" fairy tale will say to the child way that "animism" is not a solution. At a certain point, the fairy tale that personifies the table, the lamp, and the bed will appear similar, in the symbolizing mechanism, to the game in which the child has imaginative control over things—a "doing as if" which does not obligate the child to respect the properties of the objects. It will be up to the child to conceive the opposition of "real versus imaginary," "really true versus true for the game," that permits him to grasp reality.

3) I shall reflect upon the actual features of *the child's* "journey around the house," which is much different from *my* journey during *my* childhood.

This is a point that is worth developing.

The electric light, gas, television, washing machine, refrigerator, vacuum cleaner, hair dryer, mixer, and record player are only some of the elements of the domestic landscape that the child of today knows, and that are very different from those of the grandfather who grew up perhaps in a rustic kitchen between a stove and a water bucket. These new things tell children about a world full of machines. On all the walls there are sockets and switches, and no matter how well children know that they should not touch them, parents cannot command them not to reflect about human beings and their force, about their powers that ignite lights, and cause motors to hum and rustle, that transform hot into cold, raw into cooked, et cetera. From the balcony, children see cars, helicopters, and planes pass by. Even among their toys are machines of every kind that imitate on a small scale those in the adult world.

The outside world penetrates the house itself in many ways that were unknown to children fifty years ago. The telephone rings, and the father's voice can be heard. The dial of the radio is turned, and there are sounds, tones, and songs. The button on the TV is pushed, and the screen is filled with pictures, and with each picture there is a word that gradually becomes associated with it, and the words must be absorbed and stored, information is to be deciphered that must be approached with caution, and added to the information one already possesses.

The picture that the child of today conceives of the world is, by necessity, completely different from that which his or her father conceived, even though very few decades separate them. The child's experience places him in a position to perform diverse kinds of operations, perhaps even mental operations more complex than those of the father. It is difficult to prove this with certainty because we lack the required measurements for comparison.

In addition, the household objects provide information about the materials with which they are made, the colors with which they are painted, the forms in which they are designed (by a designer, because artisans don't exist anymore). "Reading" these objects, the child learns different things from them than the grandfather learned "reading" an oil lamp. The objects insert themselves into a different cultural model.

The great-grandmother cooked baby food for the grandfather. But it is the large industrial company that prepares the baby food for the grandchildren, who become involved in the sphere of this industry before they can leave the house on their own feet.

Thus we have much more material at our disposal to fabricate stories, and we can use a richer language. The imagination is a function of experience, and the experience of the child of today is more extensive than that of the child of yesterday. (I don't know whether I can say more intense, but that is another matter.)

At this point it would be superfluous to give examples. Each object, according to its nature, offers basic material for a story. Even I have hung some stories on the clothes rack of the imagination. For example, I have invented a Prince Ice Cream, who lives in a refrigerator. I have made a character, one who was too attached to the television, jump into the screen. I have arranged a marriage between a young man, who previously had fallen in love with a red Japanese motorcycle, and a washing machine. I have conceived a magic record that compels listeners to dance, and while they are dancing, they are robbed by two crooks, et cetera.

It is, I think, important to begin using objects with the smallest children, who already have an intimate and special relationship with them. For example, the bed. Children jump on the bed, play around there, and do everything they can so as not to go to sleep. They hate the bed if it is bedtime, for they must interrupt some important work to go to sleep. If we project this refusal onto the object, then we get:

> The story of the bed that refused to let the child sleep. The bed turned over, jumped on the ceiling, ran to the staircase landing, and fell down the stairs; the pillow wanted to lay at the foot of the bed and not under the child's head. . . . There is a motor bed that travels in distant countries in order to hunt crocodiles. . . . There is the talking bed that tells many stories. Among the stories is the one about the bed that refused to let the child sleep, et cetera.

Although we must take the nature of the object into consideration, this does not prevent us from making a more arbitrary use of it, and from taking a lesson from the child, who assigns the most incredible roles to the objects:

> A chair was running to catch the bus. It was very late and the chair ran in haste, skipping on its four legs. All of a sudden it lost one of the legs and wobbled dangerously. Fortunately a boy who was passing by was quick to pick it up and place it back on the chair. And while he was replacing the leg, the boy recommended, "You shouldn't run that way. There is plenty of time, and life is short." "Young man, let me loose. Don't make me miss the bus." And the chair began to run again, faster than before. Et cetera. This chair was a teacher, and he taught parrots how to speak. Et cetera.

These stories can be used at certain moments such as mealtimes and bedtimes, and they do not necessarily have to obey the iron laws of the sonata form, but rather those of improvisation, which are more flexible. There can be cues, fragments, zigzag stories, which begin and do not end, which overtake one another, and do not remember what they do, like monkeys in a zoo. In sum, these stories have the character of the games that children play, which are hardly ever complete but more frequently assume the form of a book that wanders among many stories, scattered with objects that are picked up, dropped, picked up again, and lost along the way.

28 • The Toy as Character

BETWEEN THE WORLD of toys and the adult world there is a relationship more ambiguous than it would seem at first sight. On the one hand, toys come into existence "through decline," on the other, through conquest. Certain things that were at one time important in the adult world accept being reduced to toys so they do not vanish when their time has passed. Thus the bow and arrow, having ceased to count on the battlefields, resigned themselves to becoming instruments of play. Masks, under our very eyes, stopped playing their role in the adult Carnival celebrations and became a monopoly of children. Dolls and spinning tops were sacred and ritualistic objects before they had to settle for becoming toys for children. But even more banal objects can fall from their daily pedestals. An old broken alarm clock, reduced to a toy, can also experience this decline as a promotion. The trunks forgotten in an attic and then discovered with their hidden treasures and returned to life by children, have they fallen or risen in our estimation?

Thanks to the imagination of children, things, animals, and machines become toys by virtue of the changes the children make. Various arts, crafts, and professions become play. Certainly, the toy industry manufactures small trains, cars, doll clothes, and chemistry sets for the "little scientist" in an incessant process to make the adult world into a miniature one that does not forget to include mini-tanks and mini-missiles. But the need of the child to imitate the adult is not an invention of industry. It is not an ignorant demand. Rather, it is part of the child's desire to grow.

The world of toys is thus a composite world. As such, it also comprises the attitude of the child toward the toy. On the one hand, children obey the world's stimulations, learning how to use the toy for the intended game, and discovering all the other ways that it can be put to use. On the other hand, children use it as a means to express themselves, almost as though entrusting it to represent their personal dramas. The toy is the world that they want to conquer and with which they measure themselves (hence the impulse to take the toy apart to see how it is made; or to destroy it). But it is also a projection, an extension of the self.

The girl who plays with her dolls and with their trousseau of clothes, furniture, utensils, plates, cups, electrical household machines, and miniature homes and villages, recapitulates in the game all her knowledge of domestic life, and she practices how to handle objects, to take them apart and to put them back together, to assign them a space and a role. But at the same time, she uses the dolls for dramatizing her own relations and, if necessary, her conflicts. She scolds her doll with the same words with which she has been scolded by her mother, in order to project on it any sense of guilt she may have. She fondles and caresses it to express her need for affection. She can select one doll to love and hate in a very special way if this doll embodies her little brother, whom she envies. As Piaget has written, these symbolical games constitute an "authentic way of thinking."

Often, during the game, the child has a monologue, narrating the events of the game to herself. She animates the toys, or turns away from them to follow the echoes of a word or something that she has suddenly remembered.

Apart from certain highly perceptive observations made by Francesco De Bartolomeis about the "collective monologue" of children who play together in a daycare center—*together*, in a manner of speaking, because each child plays for himself or herself, and they do not have a "dialogue" with each other, but they each have a loud monologue—it appears to me that the monologue of the child at play has never been studied the way it deserves to be. I think that a study of this kind would tell us many things about the relationship between child and toy that we still do not know, and would be most essential for a grammar of the imagination. I am certain that due to our lack of attention hundreds of inventions have been irretrievably lost.

How many words does a child who plays with building blocks pronounce in an hour? What kind of words? To what degree do the words pertain to the project, the strategy, and the tactics of the game, and to what degree do they diverge from them? What pieces unexpectedly become characters, receive a name, begin to act on their own accord, and have personal adventures? What associations of ideas are revealed in the course of the game? What significant hidden secrets could we attribute to the gestures, processes of symbolization, and distribution of each piece, if we pay careful attention? We know only—because patient scientists have proven it through experiments—that boys tend to construct things in a vertical way; girls, on the other hand, tend to enclose a space. Such a connection between the structure of the imagination and one's biological structure is for us lay people fascinating and at the same time incredible. But it amounts to very little with respect to what one would like to know.

Inventing stories with toys is almost natural. It is something that comes about almost by itself if one plays with children. The story is nothing but an extension, a development, a joyous explosion of the toy. All parents are aware of this if they have found the time to play with their children and their dolls, blocks, or little cars. This kind of activity is something that should be obligatory for every parent—and, certainly, it's entirely possible.

When adults play with a child, they have an advantage because they have a wider field of experience. Therefore, they can create more space with their imaginations. This is why children like to have parents as playmates. For example, if they construct something together, the adult has a better idea of how to estimate proportions and how to balance things. The adult possesses a richer repertoire of forms to imitate, et cetera. The game is enriched, gains in organization and duration, and opens up new horizons.

The point here does not concern playing in place of the child, who becomes relegated to the humiliating role of spectator. But it concerns how an adult can place himself or herself at the child's service. It is the child who commands. The adult plays with children in order to stimulate their capacity to invent things, to place new instruments in their hands so that they will use them when they are alone, and to teach them how to play. There is talk during the game. One learns from the child to speak to the pieces of the game, to assign them names and roles, to transform an error into an invention, a gesture into a story, using what Jerome Bruner (*On Knowing: Essays for the Left Hand*) calls "the liberty to be dominated by the object." But also, one learns—just as the child does—to entrust the pieces with secret messages because they tell the child how much we love him or her, that he or she can count on us, that our strength is theirs.

Thus a "little theater" originates in the game in which the teddy bear and mini-crane, the little houses and the little machines act, friends and relatives take the stage, and fairy tale characters appear and disappear.

In this game the children and adults can also become bored if the toy is restricted and limited to its technical role, is rapidly explored and rapidly exhausted. Changes of scenes, sensational scenes, and leaps into the absurd that favor discovery are all necessary.

Adults who are open-minded will not become tired of learning the essential principles of "dramatization" from the children. And then it is up to adults to raise this dramatization to a higher and more stimulating level than the little inventor can with his or her powers that remain weak and limited.

29 • Marionettes and Puppets

WITHOUT BEING PRECISE, the term *little theater* in the last chapter alluded to marionettes and puppets. Here they will take center stage in person, those fascinating little people. But I shall not add anything to this vague definition, for it would never occur to me to compete with Goethe and Kleist, who wrote remarkable essays about their own fascination with them.

I was a puppeteer three times in my life—as a child in an alcove beneath the stairs with a window built to serve as the opening for the stage; as a teacher for my pupils in a village school on the banks of Lake Maggiore (I remember that one of the children, when he went to confession, told the entire confession with questions and answers in his notebook, which he called "Open Diary"); and finally as a grown man for some weeks before an audience of farmers who gave me gifts of eggs and sausages. Puppeteer, the most wonderful profession in the world.

If one disregards the philosophical details concerning marionettes and puppets, we can see that they came to children through a double "decline." Their most distant ancestors are the ritual masks of primitive tribes. The first fall was from the sacred to the profane, from ritual to theater. The second fall, from the theater to the world of games. This is a history that has developed before our very eyes. Who in Italy has resisted the decline and maintained the tradition of this extraordinary form of popular theater other than Otello Sarzi and a few collaborators?

Mariano Dolci, who worked for a long time with Sarzi and who wrote a valuable practical handbook, *I burattini—strumento pedagogico per la scuola* (*Puppets—Pedagogical Instrument for the School*) for the cultural bureau of the city of Reggio Emilia (Where else in Italy could this happen!), commented in the following way on the decline of puppets:

> The role that these puppet theaters had in popular culture was very important, and if one leafs through the titles of the texts of plays still being produced at the beginning of the twentieth century, it is astounding to see the vast spectrum of interests that they served. We find texts treating biblical and mythological themes, adaptations of famous theatrical and literary works from all over the world, historical plays, comedies with social, political, polemical, anticlerical, and topical references, et cetera.

I was fortunate one time to see an adaptation of *Aïda* for marionettes. On the other hand, the only "important" puppet play that I can remember is: *Ginevra degli Almieri, or The Person Buried Alive, with Gioppino the Grave Robber.* I remember it because I saw it one evening when I fell in love with a girl from Cremona. I don't remember her name because it was long before my first real love, which one never forgets.

Sarzi and his friends have done a great deal for puppetry. But I believe that the most important thing they accomplished was that they began going into schools not only to perform with puppets, but to teach children how to make their own puppets and how to move them, how to construct stages, to prepare the sets, the lights, the musical accompaniment, to direct and perform. Mariano Dolci has a beautiful beard like the Fire-eater in *Pinocchio.* As soon as the children see it, they understand that they can expect something extraordinary from him. Mariano takes some round shiny buttons from a sack and teaches the children how to pin noses and eyes on them, to draw mouths, to invent characters and bodies for them, to dress them, and to slip one's finger inside. . . .

In the daycare centers of Reggio Emilia, the puppet theater is a permanent fixture in the room. At any time, a child can disappear in it, take his favorite puppet, and put it to work. If another child arrives, then two different stories are performed at the same time. The two children can decide to play together and take turns: the first is puppet A who takes the stick and hits puppet B. Then B hits A. There are children who speak only through the puppets. There are children who, when they move the croco-dile puppet, jump away quickly so that they will not be eaten. To be sure they are the ones who put their fingers in the right spot to make the artifi-cial body of the wild beast move, but one never knows. . . .

In Rome I knew a teacher by the name of Mr. Bonanno, who taught at the Badini School and died at a very young age. He had a teacher puppet in his puppet theater for his fifth graders, who said everything to the puppet that they would never dare say to their real teacher. Meanwhile their teacher sat in front of the stage and listened to everything. In this way he learned what the children really thought of him. He told me one time, "I'm learn-ing my mistakes."

Puppets can be found more often at school; marionettes, more often at home. There is a reason for this, but I do not know what it is. The most wonderful marionette theater that I know is English. It is made out of cardboard. You cut it out and mount it. Even the scenes and the figures are cutouts. It is extraordinarily flexible because it is only the basic framework for the theater, and all the rest is to be invented.

The true language of the puppets and marionettes is in their move-ment. They are not made for long monologues or dialogues. If Hamlet recites his monologue in a puppet play, there must be at the very least a devil who from time to time tries to steal the skull and to replace it with a tomato. On the other hand, a single puppet can maintain a dialogue for hours with its audience of children without tiring them, if it knows how to do this.

The advantage of the puppet theater over the marionette theater lies in the former's capacity to create better movement. The advantage of the marionette theater over the puppet theater lies in its set design and fur-nishings. Girls fill the stage with their doll clothes and accessories, and all this occupies so much time and causes so many things to happen that it is no longer necessary to perform a play.

The typical resources of both theaters are learned only through prac-tice. There is not much more to say except to recommend reading the handbook by Mariano Dolci. The question that concerns me now is: What stories can we invent for the marionettes and puppets?

The popular folk tales and their application according to the tech-niques already discussed offer a repertory that is practically inexhaustible. With one warning: the introduction of a comical character is almost obliga-tory, and will always turn out to be productive.

Two puppets chosen at random are a fantastic binominal: whoever needs further explanation can refer to the preceding chapters.

Instead of using the binominal, I would like to explore the possibility of entrusting the puppet theater with certain "secret messages," and here I would like to discuss at least two fantastic exercises.

The first consists in making use of the material offered by television. That is, it does not take much to create an alternative or a principle for a critical alternative to the purely passive reception of TV programs. The second consists in attributing hidden roles to certain characters. I shall explain both points in more detail.

There is practically no telecast that cannot be used as raw material for a puppet play. The point here is not to try to produce a "counter-telecast," no matter what it takes. The play will become a counter-telecast by itself through the marionettes or puppets—by their movements, their capacity to reduce everything to the absurd and to ridicule the character of the conceited host of the TV show, the howling singer, the quiz show contestants, the infallible detective, or the lurking TV monster. It is merely sufficient to bring about a comparison between the characters of a TV program and an incongruous person: Pinocchio appearing on the TV news show, a witch in the Zorro series, a devil on the morning show.

Once, when I visited an elementary school, I saw the "Wheel of Fortune" quiz show with the devil as a contestant. Just a short time before this I had in fact told the students a story about a crocodile who appears on a TV show and eats the "Wheel of Fortune" host. The children did not have a crocodile among their puppets, but a devil. Using the devil as their "key," their story had a greater comic effect than mine.

For the second exercise, let us return to the smallest children in the family. What the fifth graders did with their teacher, speaking to him via the teacher-puppet, we can do with our younger children, speaking to them via marionettes. It is necessary to bear in mind that in some way the marionettes lend themselves to creating permanent identities. The king, no matter what he does, is fundamentally the father, the authority figure, the power, the adult, whom one needs but whom one may fear, who oppresses children but also protects them from any kind of harm. The queen is the mother. The prince is the boy, the princess is the girl. The fairy is "the beautiful thing," the good magic, hope, satisfaction, the future. The devil embodies all the fears, the lurking monsters, all kinds of enemies. If we remember these analogies, then we can charge the puppets—while they act out their adventures—with transmitting reassuring messages to the children. Communicating through symbols is no less important than communicating through words. Sometimes it is the only mode of communication with children.

Since I have never had any experience in this, I do not know to what degree children can accept a marionette representing them, bearing their names, acting for them in the puppet theater. It may be that children would accept the game as they accept the story in which they figure as protagonists. But it may be that they would reject an identification because it is so public and because it is with an object that is exact, visible, and palpable. Children, too, care about their secrets. (*Auch Kinder haben Geheimnisse* [*Children, Too, Have Their Secrets*] is the title of a book published by Hans Stempel and Martin Ripkins.)

30 · The Child as Protagonist

"ONCE UPON A TIME there was a boy who was called Charlie."

"Like me?"

"Like you."

"It was me."

"Yes, it was you."

"What did I do?"

"That is what I'm going to tell you now."

In this classic dialogue between a mother and son, there is the first explanation for the wonderful tense in Italian called the "imperfect," which children use to begin a game.

"I was the guard, and you escaped."

"You cried out. . . ."

It is like a curtain that opens when a play commences. In my opinion, the use of the imperfect tense originates from the beginning of fairy tales: "Once upon a time there was. . . ." But there are other explanations about the imperfect tense, and I refer you to the notes at the end of this book (see "A Verb for Playing").

Most mothers tell stories in which their child is the protagonist. That corresponds to and satisfies the child's egocentrism. But the mothers have a purpose that suits their own didactic goals.

"Charlie was a child who knocked over the salt . . . who did not want to drink milk . . . who did not want to go to bed. . . ."

It is a shame to adopt the imperfect of the fairy tale and games for the purpose of warning and intimidating children. It is almost like using a gold watch to dig holes in the sand.

"Charlie was a great traveler. He traveled around the world and saw monkeys, lions. . . ."

"Did I also see elephants?"

"Also elephants."

"And giraffes?"

"Also giraffes."

"And little donkeys?"

"Certainly."

"And then what?"

This way seems better to me. The game becomes much more fruitful if we use it to put children in delightful situations, to let them accomplish memorable deeds, and to present them with a future of fulfillment and rewards, told in a fairy tale. I know quite well that the future will not be as beautiful as it is in a fairy tale. But that is not what counts. When they are little, children must stock up on optimism and trust for the challenge of life. And then, we must not underestimate the educational value of utopia. If we did not trust in a better world despite it all, what would make us go to the dentist?

If the real Charlie is afraid of the dark, the Charlie of the fairy tale wasn't at all afraid of it. He did what nobody had courage to do. He went where nobody dared to go. . . .

In this type of story the mother portrays the child's own experience and person objectively to that child. She helps him to clarify his position among things and to grasp the situations in which he plays a central role.

In order to know oneself one must be able to imagine oneself.

The point here is not to encourage children to have empty fantasies (if we accept—and this is not conceded by psychoanalysts—that there can be such a thing as absolutely empty fantasies that do not refer to anything substantial), but to give children a hand so that they can imagine themselves and imagine their own destinies.

"Charlie was a shoemaker and made the most splendid shoes in the world. He was an engineer and built the longest, highest, and sturdiest bridges in the world."

At three years of age, at five years, these are not "forbidden dreams," they are indispensable exercises.

In order to ring more "true," stories with the child as protagonist must definitely have their private side. A certain uncle of the child or a certain neighbor must enter the story, and it cannot be someone else. At key points in the story, the places must be places that the child can recognize. The words must be loaded with familiar allusions. It is, therefore, useless to provide models.

Frequently, older children also like to be part of stories, even if only their names are involved. When I went to schools to tell stories, I often gave characters the names of the children who were listening to my tale. I changed the place names and used places that the children knew. The names reinforced the children's interest and attention because they stimulated the mechanism of identification.

And this mechanism—which is always present in every reader, film spectator, or TV viewer—is what permits the introduction of "messages" into the story with the certitude that they will arrive at their destination.

31 · "Taboo" Stories

I PERSONALLY find it useful to tell to children a certain group of "taboo" stories, but other people would wrinkle their noses at them. These stories represent an attempt to have a discussion with children about subjects that interest them intimately, but which traditional education generally relegates to that class of things about which "it is better not to speak." They involve the bodily functions and children's sexual curiosity. Of course, this definition of "taboo" is polemical, for I am calling for the breaking of taboos.

I believe that we must be able to speak about these things in complete freedom not only in the family but in the school, and we should not just use scientific terms, because people do not live by science alone. I also know the troubles that some teachers have—whether in kindergarten, elementary, or middle school—if they want to bring the children to express themselves bluntly, to free themselves from fears, to defeat any eventual sense of guilt. The part of public opinion that respects the taboos is quick to make accusations of obscenity, to have the school authorities intervene, and to wave the rules and regulations manual in their hands. If a child dares to draw a nude, male or female, with all parts of the body, then it does not take much before stupidity, cruelty, and fear of sexuality explode against the child's teacher. But how many teachers recognize the freedom of their pupils to write the word *shit*, if it is necessary?

In this respect, popular folk tales are sublimely above hypocrisy of this kind. In their narrative freedom, these tales do not hesitate to make use of what is called scatological vocabulary to provoke laughter considered indecent, to report clearly about sexual relations, et cetera. Can we appropriate this laughter in a manner so that it is not indecent but emancipatory? I honestly believe we can.

We know how important it is for the growing child to learn how to control his or her bodily functions. Psychoanalysis has truly rendered us a service by teaching us that there is intense and delicate emotional function associated with this control. Aside from this, every family is confronted a long time with the phase in which the child has very special relations to the potty, whereby the family members are drawn into the rituals attending the process. And there are threats if the child doesn't "go," promises if the child decides to "go," rewards and praise if he or she has "gone." And whatever the child produces after he or she has "gone" is proudly displayed as proof of his or her skill. There are attentive inspections, conversations among adults about the meaning of certain signs, consultations with the doctor, telephone calls to the aunt who knows everything. It is, therefore, not at all astonishing if, in the life of the infant, the potty and whatever is connected to it assume an almost dramatic meaning for years to come. But they are also filled with contradictory and mysterious associations. Indeed, one cannot speak freely about such an important thing, much less joke about it.

If adults want to say that something is not good, should not be touched or watched, they say that it is "shit." Around this "shit," a world of things originates, and these things are suspicious, prohibited, and perhaps sinful. Tensions, worries, and nightmares arise. Without knowing it, adults carry these things inside themselves like mysterious objects in a forbidden room. But they can at least search and find compensation in the comical aspect of dirty stories, the obscene, and the forbidden. Indeed, adults are even more versed in the repertory of the jokes that are not to be told in the presence of children, and that sales representatives spread from city to city and country to country, just like the merchants of long ago used to spread stories of marvelous events or legends of the saints. Children are forbidden to enjoy the laughter evoked by these stories. But, in fact, children really have more need of this than adults. . . .

There is nothing like laughter to help children defuse tension and to bring about balance in their lives, to leave the prison of disturbing impressions and neurotic theorizing. There is a period during which it is almost requisite for adults to invent stories about "poop," "potty," and other similar things, for children and with children. I have done this. I know many other parents who have done this, and they do not regret it.

Among my memories as a father without taboos—at least in this respect—there are many rhymes and songs about these themes that I have stored up and improvised with the children of my relatives. We sang songs in the car—I don't know what the conditioned impulse was—Sunday mornings (in the evening the children were too tired to sing). If I were not more or less a prisoner of conventions, as we all are, I would have included these "poop songs" in my collections of children's rhymes. I believe that only after the year 2000 will there be authors courageous enough to do this. . . .

Car trips had a direct influence on my *Storia del Re Mida* (*The Story of King Midas*). After he is freed from the gift of changing everything he touches into gold, he is compelled by mischance to transform everything that he touches into "poop," and the first thing that he touches is his car. . . .

This little story has nothing special about it, but when I go into a school, the children often ask me to tell it, and I sense a sneaky delight creep into the classroom. The children want to hear me pronounce the word *poop*, letter for letter, and as they laugh at a certain point, it becomes very clear that the poor children have never been able to give vent to their feelings and to pronounce the word themselves as much as they would like.

One morning I was in the country with a group of children from our extended family, and we invented an entire scatological novel that lasted for hours and was an extraordinary success. What was also extraordinary was that after we had laughed until we thought our stomachs would burst, nobody alluded to this story any more. The "novel" had fulfilled its function: the contesting of all that was considered decent was carried to an extreme, and thereby all the aggression was exhausted. For those who may be interested, the plot was as follows:

In Tarquinia certain incidents of a particular kind occur. One day a vase falls from a balcony and almost kills a pedestrian. Another day the gutter of the roof breaks loose and damages a car. . . . All this always happens near a certain house. . . . Always at a certain time. . . . Is it magic? The evil eye? After careful investigation, a retired teacher succeeds in discovering that the disasters occurred in direct relation with the "potty time" of a certain Maurice, three and a half years old. Many joyful events could be attributed to the influence of the potty, however, such as winning the lottery and the discovery of Etruscan treasures. In brief: the various events—fortunate or fateful—depended on the form, quantity, consistency, and color of Maurice's poop. The secret does not remain one for long. First, members of the family, then other groups, friends and enemies, intervene to direct the course of events. Intrigues and conspiracies are developed around the nourishment of Maurice. The ends justify the means. . . . Rival bands fight for control over Maurice's bowel movements in order to realize their different projects. Bribery of the doctor, the pharmacist, and the maid. . . . A German professor, who is on vacation in Tarquinia and informed about these things, decides to write a scientific study that will bring fame and fortune, but due to a foolhardy purge of his own system he is transformed into a horse and flees to the marshes of Maremma, followed by his secretary. (Unfortunately I do not remember the end of this story that takes on cosmic dimensions, nor do I feel like inventing one on the spur of the moment.)

If one day I write down this story, I shall consign the manuscript to a lawyer and indicate that it should not be published until the year 2017, when the concept of "bad taste" will have undergone a necessary and inevitable evolution. By that time it will be considered "bad taste" to exploit the work of others and to lock up innocent people and children in prison. Children, instead, will be free to think up truly educational stories, even ones about "poop."

In daycare centers, in which children are really free to invent stories and to talk about things that count, they go through a phase in which they make use of so-called bad language in an aggressive, almost obsessive manner. The story in the next chapter documents this phase. It was told by a five-year-old child in the Diana Daycare Center in Reggio Emilia and was transcribed by the teacher, Giulia Notari.

32 • Peter and the Putty

One time Peter was playing with some putty. A priest passes by and asks him, "What are you doing?"
"I'm making a priest like you."
A cowboy comes by and asks, "What are you doing?"
"I'm making a cowboy like you."
An Indian passes by and asks him, "What are you doing?"
"I'm making an Indian like you."
A devil passes by, and he was good but then he becomes bad because Peter throws "poop" at him. The devil cries because he was covered with shit. But then he becomes good again.

What is most striking in this splendid story is the use of scatological language in an emancipatory way. The child, who is in a position to express himself without fear of censorship due to the non-repressive surroundings, is quick to make use of this freedom for his own purposes—that is, to exorcize the sense of guilt connected with his bodily functions. The point here concerns the "forbidden words," which are "not good," which one is "not supposed to say," according to the family values. If one pronounces these words, then this act signifies a refusal to submit to repressive standards and a desire to turn the sense of guilt into something ridiculous.

Through this outburst a more comprehensive process of self-liberation from fear, all kinds of fear, takes place. The child personifies his enemies and all that he knows about guilt and threat; he plays one enemy against the other and takes pleasure in humiliating them.

It should be noted that the process is not all that linear. At the beginning, the devil is approached with a certain caution. It is a "good" devil. One never knows. The exorcism implied in the flattering adjective is enormously reinforced by the gesture: in order to banish the devil, "poop" is thrown upon him, that is, in a way that is the opposite of baptismal water. But it also happens in dreams that an object represents its opposite, isn't it true? (Dr. Freud approves.)

Now the devil has lost his reassuring mask of goodness. He is what he is—"evil." But this recognition occurs when evil is challenged and ridiculed because he is completely besmirched: "covered with shit."

The "laugh of superiority" that permits the child to triumph over the devil also allows him to reestablish himself. From the moment that the child does not have any more fear, the devil can become "good" once again, but at the level of a marionette. It was a real devil that the child had bombarded with excrement. Now the devil has been given a new dimension, reduced to a toy. One can forgive him . . . perhaps because, by doing this, the child, too, will be forgiven for using "dirty words"? There is a certain uneasiness that remains, or a revenge of the internal censor that the story was not able to overthrow completely. . . .

This reading, which refers back to the remarks that I made in the previous chapter, does not, however, provide a complete explanation of the story. And since we have reached this point, we might as well undertake one.

Speaking about the creative process in literature, Roman Jakobson observed that "the poetic function projects the principle of equivalence of the axis of selection (verbal) on to the axis of combination." For example, the rhyme can do extraordinary things with tone and impose itself on the discourse: the sound precedes the meaning. As we have already seen, this occurs when children invent stories. But in the story of "Peter and the Putty," the axis of personal experience is projected before the "axis of verbal selection"—in this specific case, the game with the putty and the very manner in which it is experienced by the child. The story assumes, in fact, the form of the "monologue" that the child brings to the play of molding figures. It is the *form*, not the *material*, that is the putty in the game, before the words are inserted. By contrast, in the story the material of expression is constituted by the words.

In sum, the language assumes its full symbolic function in the story and rejects the material framework of the game. Perhaps the point here is that the child's relationship to reality is less rich than the child's relationship to the actual game itself? Must we consider that the game is more concretely formative in its fundamental ambiguity of game-work, while the story, as a verbal game of fantasy, would be a form of escape? I don't really think so. On the contrary, the story appears to me to be a more advanced phase of mastery over the real, a freer relationship with the materials. It is a moment of reflection that goes beyond the game. It is already a form of rationalization of experience—an introduction to abstraction.

In the game with the putty (Plasticine, clay, and other similar materials) the child has only one antagonist—the material with which he works. In the story he can multiply the antagonists, and he can do things with the words that he cannot do with the putty. . . .

In regard to the putty, there are other references, articulated in the story, and they are connected to the experience of the child, to the people of his world and the characters of his myth. These references appear to us joined in pairs, according to the "thought of the pairs" illustrated by Wallon (and also according to the principle of the fantastical binominal). The putty is opposed to poop, which recalls the putty through coincidental analogies that were undoubtedly discovered and tested by the child during the game—form, color, et cetera. (Who knows how many times the child molded poop with the putty?) The cowboy is immediately opposed to and joined with the Indian. The priest with the devil.

It is true that the devil does not appear immediately in the story, but only later, after a significant delay. One could say that the child decided, just as he thought up the priest or right after, to put the priest aside to construct the final effect. . . . In reality, the child could have left him out from the beginning in order to include in the story the less menacing figures of the cowboy and Indian. . . . Fear tore apart the "priest-devil" pair as it arose. . . . Later, the child had to come to terms with the feared image, and so he found a way to introduce the devil into the story so he could banish and ridicule him.

But we cannot overlook the possibility—if we take into account the axis of verbal selection—that the letters *d-i-a* of Indian may have been the decisive spark for evoking the "devil" (in Italian the word for devil is *diavolo*) and bringing about the suggestion for the pair.

As we have seen, the devil himself is split into a "good devil" and a "bad devil." And in a parallel way, "poop," too, is split—it is called "poop" the first time, but the second time it is called "shit." The child's name grows into a more "daring" adult name that testifies to the growing ("crescendo") security with which the child's imagination handles its story. The self-confidence of the child grows with free expression.

Moreover, in this particular child it is possible that the "crescendo" has something to do with his musical inclination. There are clues of this in his choice of words as well as in the structure of his story.

Notice the use of the initial letter *p* (or fully in *p major*): Peter, putty, passes by, poop, priest. What is this predilection? Is it the word *papa* that appears each time and each time is rejected? There may be something to this. But it may also be that it is the ear that insists on this alliteration as a simple musical theme—that it is really the *p* that makes the "priest" to "pass by" at first. In sum, first it is the sound, then the character, as it happens many times in poetical processes (reread this last phrase—you will see me carried away by *p* . . .).

Also the expression *good devil* demands an explanation, although the psychologist might not feel it needs one. In my opinion this good devil is not the child's original invention but the echo of conversations in the family, the memory of a popular metaphor that defines a good devil as a good-hearted person, modest and incapable of doing any evil. The child could have heard this expression at home and retained it, but he interpreted it literally, though not without some confusion and perplexity ("If the devil is bad, how can he do good?"). However, the creative process can also be nurtured in the poet by such confusion and ambiguity, as it can in the child or in anyone. The little narrator took the metaphor and inverted the terms in it: "good devil." The parallel with the musical process is once again apparent.

As far as the structure goes, the story appears to be divided into two distinct parts, each having a three-part rhythm:

First Part
1) the priest
2) the cowboy
3) the Indian
Second Part
1) the good devil
2) the bad devil
3) the good devil

The first part is more analytical. Here the melody, so to speak, is simply repeated three times, according to the scheme A-B.

A. What are you doing?
B. I'm making a priest like you.
A. What are you doing?
B. I'm making a cowboy like you.
A. What are you doing?
B. I'm making an Indian like you.

The second part is faster and more animated with its non-verbal but physical clash between the child and the passerby, the devil.

First an *andantino* then an *allegro presto*. There is an instinctive sense of rhythm that clearly presides in this configuration.

I must report here, more from scruple than from necessity, about an objection that I heard made against this story. In the encounter with the devil, the putty is no longer present, and this would seem to deprive the story of logic and the conclusion of the soothing harmony that everyone expects.

But none of this is true. The putty and the poop are the same. The child could have explained later that the putty Peter threw on the devil really seemed to be something else and that the devil, in his ignorance, mistook it for something else. But that explanation would have seemed somewhat pedantic.

The child condensed the two images: his imagination condensed them for him according to the law of "oneiric (dreamlike) condensation," which I have already discussed. There can be no mistake. The logic of the imagination can be declared as fully satisfied.

It should be clear by now that the story is made up of diverse parts: the words—their sounds, their meanings, their unexpected relations; the personal memories; the surfacing of the unconscious; the pressures of the censor. Everything is combined in a process that has provided the child with intense satisfaction. The imagination was the instrument, but the entire personality of the child was involved in the creative act.

Unfortunately, in judging children's creative work, the school commonly restricts its attention to the level of spelling, grammar, and syntax, which does not even begin to touch the real linguistic level, not to mention the complex world of content. The fact is that children's writing is read at school only to grade and classify it, not to understand it. The sieve of correctness collects and assesses the pebbles, letting the gold, however, seep through.

33 • Stories for Laughing

THE CHILD WHO SEES his mother put the spoon into her ear instead of her mouth laughs because the mother "makes a mistake." She is so big and yet does not know how to use the spoon in the proper way, according to society's rules. This "laugh of superiority" (see *Il senso del comico nel fanciullo* [*The Child's Sense of the Comic*] by Raffaele La Porta) is among the first forms of laughter the child is capable of. The fact that the mother commits the mistake intentionally does not make the least difference: her gesture is in any case a wrong gesture. If the mother repeats this gesture two or three times and then varies it by sticking the spoon in her eye, the laugh of superiority will be reinforced by a laugh of surprise. These highly simple mechanisms have been carefully noted by the inventors of cinematic gags. Moreover, a psychologist will observe that even the laugh of superiority is an instrument of knowledge that plays on the opposition between *correct use* and *incorrect use* of the spoon.

The simplest way to invent comical stories is to take advantage of errors. The very first stories were more like gestures than verbal expressions. Papa puts the shoes on his hands. He puts the shoes on his head. He wants to eat soup with a hammer. . . . Oh, if only Giacomo's father, Monaldo Leopardi, had made a little use of the clown for the benefit of his little son, there, in his home, then perhaps as a grown-up poet he would have shown his gratitude and honored him by writing a poem about him. Instead we had to wait for Camillo Sbarbaro in order to experience a father made out of flesh and bones in poetry.

Little Giacomo sits in his high chair and is intent on eating his cereal. The door bursts open, and in walks his stately father the count, disguised as a farmer. He is playing the flute and . . . dancing a jig. . . . Oh, get out of here, noble father, you haven't understood a thing. . . .

It is from such mistaken gestures that the so-called proper stories themselves originate, and in turn they provide whole phalanges of mistaken characters:

> Mr. So-and-So goes to a shoemaker to have a pair of shoes made for his hands. He is a man who walks on his hands. He eats with his feet and plays the harmonium with them. He is a topsy-turvy man. He reverses everything when he speaks. He calls bread "water" and suppository pills "lemon drops."

> A dog does not know how to bark. It believes that a cat can teach it how to do this, but naturally the cat teaches the dog how to meow. He goes to a cow and learns mooing: moooo! . . .

A horse wants to learn how to type on a typewriter. It destroys dozens of machines with its hooves. A machine as large as a house must be made for the horse. Then it writes by galloping over the keys.

It is important to pay attention to a particular aspect of the laugh of superiority, which, if we do not watch out, can assume a conservative function and align itself with the most dull and sinister conformism. Here we have the origins of a certain kind of "reactionary comic" that ridicules the new and the unusual, such as the man who wants to learn how to fly like the birds, women who want to enter politics, or people who do not speak and think like the others as custom and rules demand. . . . In order for the laugh to have a positive function, it is necessary for its arrows to target the old ideas, the fear of change, the bigotry of the norm. The non-conformist topsy-turvy characters in our stories must be successful. Their refusal to obey nature or the norms must be rewarded. Those who are "disobedient" are the ones who make the world move forward.

One type of topsy-turvy characters is represented by their comical names. "Mr. Potholder lived in a country called Pot." In this case, the name itself gives rise to the story; at the same time, the banal meaning of the common noun is amplified and assumes a more noble aspect as a proper noun. A character called Pimpom, to give a little example, is certainly funnier than one called Carl. At least at the beginning. Then we shall see what comes later.

Surprise comic effects can be achieved by animating the metaphors of language. Viktor Shklovsky already noted that some of the erotic stories in *The Decameron* are nothing but extensions of popular metaphors used to define sexual acts (in Italian, "to send the devil to hell," "the nightingale," and other similar ones). In our contemporary language we use many worn-out metaphors like old shoes. When we speak about a clock and say that it "strikes on the hour," we do not show any surprise because we have already used and heard this image used hundreds of times.

For a child, this can be something new in a situation in which "to strike" really means "to destroy," as in "striking a person or a tree down."

Once upon a time there was a clock that struck on the minute. It also struck wood and stone. It destroyed everything.

(And look at what we have here: through mere association, the non-sense took on the meaning of a parable about Father Time, who strikes down everything in his way.)

If we trip over a stone by mistake, while playing football, and experience a hard fall to the ground, we "see stars," as one says, but not like astronauts. This expression can also lead to interesting developments:

> Once upon a time there was a king who liked to look at the stars. It pleased him so much that he wanted to see them also during the day. But how could he do this? The court doctor advises him to use a hammer. The king tries to hit himself on the head with the hammer, and indeed, he "sees stars" in broad daylight. But he does not like this method. Instead, he wants the court astronomer to take the hammer and hit himself on the head so that he can describe the stars he sees to the king.
>
> "Oww! . . . I see a green comet with a violet tail. . . . Oww! I see new stars that are coming like the Three Wise Men. . . ."
>
> The astronomer flees to a distant land. The king, perhaps inspired by Massimo Bontempelli, decides to follow the stars in their course: every day he circles the earth so that he can live at night beneath the star-studded sky. His court is now on a jet plane. . . .

Our daily language and vocabulary are filled with metaphors waiting to be taken literally, at their word, and developed into a story. All the more so because many other common words still reveal themselves to the child's ear, as intact as the original metaphor.

A very productive method for comical stories is that of placing a banal character in an extraordinary context (or the other way around, putting an extraordinary person in a banal context). This method exists in almost all inventive processes. From a comic perspective, one can make full use of this potential for surprise and the deviation from the norm.

The introduction of a talking crocodile into a TV quiz show is an example. Another good example is the well-known joke about the horse that goes into a bar and asks for a beer. (The joke becomes more complicated as it is pushed to the extreme: the bartender is astonished when the horse drinks beer and eats the glass, but then throws away the handle. "That's the best part," says the bartender, and thus the story takes a subtle turn into the absurd. But this does not concern us here.) As an exercise, let us use a young chicken instead of a horse and a butcher shop instead of a bar.

> One morning a young chicken enters a butcher shop and, without waiting her turn, asks for mutton chops. The other customers become upset: What poor manners! She has no respect! She should go to the end of the line. Et cetera. . . .
>
> But the butcher's assistant serves the young chicken right away. In just those few seconds required to weigh the mutton chops, he falls in love with

her. So he asks the Mother Hen for the young chicken's hand in marriage, and they get married. Now, during the wedding celebration that is to be described, the young chicken withdraws for a moment to lay a fresh egg for her husband.

(This is not an anti-feminist story; it is just the opposite, if it is conceived in the right way.)

Children are very quick to take advantage of this method. They generally use it to "desacralize" or mock the various types of authority they are compelled to obey. They plop down the teacher in a tribe of cannibals, into a cage at the zoo, or into a chicken coop. If the teacher is intelligent, he or she will be amused by this. If the teacher isn't, he or she will be enraged. Too bad.

The complete and radical reversal of norms is also a method that is simple to use and a favorite of children. Here we have Peter—but I have already talked about him and used him as a double with Marco and Mirko in another context—who instead of being afraid of ghosts and vampires, pursues them, torments them, and throws them into a garbage can.

In this case, the exorcism of the fear ends in a "laugh of aggression"— that is very much related to those popular cake-throwing battle scenes in silent films—and a "laugh of cruelty." Children are always prone to laugh like this, but this laughter carries a certain danger with it (as when children laugh at physically disabled people, torture cats, or tear the wings off flies).

Experts have explained that people tend to laugh at somebody who falls because that person does not behave according to human norms but according to the norms of a ball. If we take this observation literally, we arrive at the method of "reification":

a) Robert's uncle is by profession a coat rack. He stands in the lobby of an expensive hotel. The customers hang hats and coats on his arms and put umbrellas and canes in his pockets. . . .

b) Mr. Dagobert is by profession a desk. When the director of the factory makes his rounds, Mr. Dagobert walks by his side and bends his back when the director must write down notes. . . .

The laugh, initially cruel, yields gradually to an uneasy feeling. The situation is comic, but unjust. One laughs, but it is a sad laugh. We have now entered the domain where Pirandello's notion of humor and his kind of play reign. And we shall stop here in order not to complicate our discussion.

34 • The Mathematics of Stories

THE FAMOUS FAIRY TALE of *The Ugly Duckling* by Hans Christian Andersen—the story about the swan who happens to land by mistake among a flock of ducks—can be expressed in mathematical terms as the adventure of an element A, which by chance lands among the elements B, where it does not find peace until it returns to its natural environment, namely to the other elements A.

The fact that Andersen did not think in terms of quantitative analysis is not important. It is also not very significant that it probably never occurred to him to play with the classifications of Linnaeus, which he knew of. He had something else in mind—above all, a parable about his own life and his development from "ugly duckling" to the swan of Denmark. But the mind is a whole, and there is not one corner in it that can remain untouched by mental processes and activity, no matter what is intended. Without realizing it, the tale is also an exercise of logic. And it is difficult to draw a clear boundary between the operations of the logic of imagination and those of pure logic.

Thus when children hear or read the tale, they move from attraction to enthusiasm, and finally to a secure promise of victory, envisioned in the destiny of the ugly duckling. In the process, they are unaware of the fact that the tale plants the seed of a logical structure in their minds, but it does.

Now we are faced with the following question: Is it legitimate to take the opposite path, to depart from a rational calculation to find a fairy tale, to use a logical structure for an invention of the imagination? I think so.

Let's say I tell children the story of a lost chick that goes in search of its mother and at first believes to have rediscovered her as a cat ("Mama!"—"Meow, get out of here, or I'll eat you!"). Then it thinks its mother is a cow, a motorcycle, and a tractor, and finally it encounters the mother hen that had been looking all over for it. She vents her anxiety by slapping the chick four times (and these slaps are, indeed, gratefully received). Here I tap into one of children's most profound needs, which is to have the assurance that they will be found by their mothers. Before they hear the comforting end of the story, I make them re-live the tension that arises from their fears of losing their parents. I touch certain mechanisms of laughter. But at the same time I set in motion an essential mental process that allows for the formation of cognitive tools. While children listen, they are practicing how to classify all possible quantitative factors, to exclude all the impossible quantitative factors of animals and objects. As they listen, imagination and reason merge into a whole, and we are not in a position to predict whether they will retain the entire story for a long time or whether it will become a certain emotion or a certain attitude toward reality.

In this context, there is another story that I like to tell children. I call it The Game of Who I Am.

A boy asks his mother, "Who am I?"

"You are my son," answers the mother.

When asked the same question, another person gives a different answer: "You are my grandson," the grandfather will say. "My brother," the brother will say. "A pedestrian, a bicyclist," the policeman will say. "My friend," the friend will say. The exploration of the quantitative relations is an exciting adventure for the child. He discovers that he is son, grandson, brother, friend, pedestrian, bicyclist, reader, student, football player. That is, he discovers his numerous relations to the world. The fundamental operation he performs is that of ordering things in a logical way. Here his emotions constitute a reinforcement of these relations.

I know teachers who invent the most wonderful stories, and help children to invent them as well, by using "logical blocks," the structural materials for arithmetic, the ciphers for quantitative analysis. In this process, the children make them into characters and attribute imaginative roles to them. This is not "another way" of doing quantitative analysis, in opposition to the usual method taught in the early grades of elementary school. It is the same way as always, but enriched in meaning. This enrichment can enable children to develop not only their capacity to grasp things with their hands, but also, just as importantly, to grasp things with the imagination.

Basically, then, the story about the blue triangle that searches for his home between the red squares, the yellow triangles, the green circles, et cetera is once more the story of *The Ugly Duckling*, but it is re-created, re-invented, and re-lived with an emotion that gives it a personal flavor.

Another mental process, which is more difficult, is the one that necessitates grasping that $a + b = b + a$. Most children do not succeed in comprehending this equation until they are six.

Giacomo Santucci, an elementary principal in Perugia, regularly asks his pupils in first grade, "Do you have a brother?"

"Yes."

"And does your brother have a brother?"

"No" is the wonderful and resolute answer, nine out of ten times. It may be that these children have not been told enough fairy tales in which the magic wand of the fairy, or the curse of a magician, can produce certain operations and their opposite with equal facility: to change a man into a mouse, and the mouse back into a man. Stories of this kind, among other kinds, can be of great help to the mind in creating the instrument of reversibility.

Let us follow this with a story about a forlorn boy who arrives in a city from who knows where. He must take bus number three and then bus number one to arrive at the central square. He thinks he can save money if he takes bus number four $(3 + 1 = 4)$. Such a story can help children distinguish between correct addition and impossible addition. Moreover, the children will amuse themselves.

Laura Conti has written in the *Giornale dei genitori* (*Parents' Journal*) that she cultivated the following image when she was a child: "In a *small* garden there was a *large* villa, and in the *large* villa, there was a *small* room. In the *small* room there was a *large* garden. . . . " This game using the relation between large and small represents the first mastery of relativity. I think that it is valuable to invent stories in this genre, in which the protagonists are pairs of opposites: little-large, small-tall, thin-fat, et cetera.

> Once upon a time there was a little hippopotamus. And there was also a big fly. The big fly often joked around with the little hippopotamus because it was little. . . . Et cetera. (Until the fly discovers that a little hippopotamus is always much bigger than a big fly.)

We can also imagine trips "to the smallest" or "to the largest" place. There is always a character who is the smallest. There is always (this story is from Enrica Agostinelli) a fat woman, who is *much fatter* than another fat woman, who despairs because she is so fat. . . .

Another example for illustrating the relations and relativity of "few" and "many":

> A man had thirty cars. People said: "Oh, he has so *many cars!*" . . . This man also had thirty hairs on his head. And the people said: "Oh, he has *very few hairs* on his head!" . . . Finally, there was nothing left for him to do but to buy a wig. Et cetera.

At the bottom of every scientific activity is measurement. There is a game for children that certainly must have been invented by a great mathematician—the game of steps. The child who orchestrates the game orders his playmates each to take "three lion steps," "three ant steps," "three crab steps," "three elephant steps," et cetera. In this way, the space for the game is continually measured and re-measured, created and recreated according to the different units of a fictive measurement.

With this game, the children can take off and create amusing mathematical exercises that help them discover "how large the classroom is by measuring shoe-lengths," "how tall Charlie is by measuring him with a spoon," "how far the table is from the oven by measuring the length with bottle tops." The step from the game to a story is short:

> At nine o'clock in the morning a child measures the shadow of a pine tree in the school courtyard: *it is thirty shoe-lengths.* A second child, who becomes curious, goes to the courtyard at one o'clock in the afternoon and repeats the measurement: the shadow is *only ten shoe-lengths long.* A discussion takes place, followed by an argument. The two boys go together to measure the shadow at two o'clock in the afternoon, and they find a third measurement. *The Mystery of the Pine Tree's Shadow* seems to me to be a perfect title for this story that can be experienced and told at the same time.

The "executive" technique (to give it a name) for inventing stories of a mathematical nature differs little from what I have already illustrated in other stories. If a character is called Mr. Tall, then his name contains his fate, and his natural character includes his adventures and misfortunes. It is enough just to analyze his name to deduce why things happen. The name represents a certain unit of measurement of the world, a special viewpoint, which has advantages and disadvantages. He has a higher vantage point than everyone else, but he often breaks down into many pieces that have to be put back together carefully. . . . Like any other toy or any other character, he presents himself as a symbol. Along the way, he can lose his mathematical origins only to acquire other meanings: it is necessary to let the imagination follow him as far as possible, without forcing him into a scheme of intentions and the intellect. In order for the story to succeed, one must always trust it and have confidence in it. Then this exercise of trust will be rewarded nine times out of ten, just as it is correctly stated in the Gospel that tells us to think of heaven and then everything will come of itself.

35 • The Child Who Listens to Fairy Tales

TO PENETRATE the experience of the child of three or four years of age, to whom the mother reads or tells fairy tales, we have very few clear facts to rely on, and thus we must make use of our own imaginations. We would be making a mistake, however, if we took the fairy tale as our point of departure: in the child's experience, the most important elements may not even be related directly to the fairy tale.

For the child, the fairy tale is above all the ideal instrument for keeping the adult nearby. The mother is always very busy. The father appears and disappears according to a mysterious rhythm that is a source of the child's recurring anxiety. The adult seldom has time to play with the child the way the child wants—that is, with complete dedication and participation and without distractions. But with the fairy tale it is different. The mother is there entirely for the child, a constant and comforting presence providing security and protection. This does not mean that if the child asks for a second tale to be told, he or she is really or exclusively interested in the events of the story. Perhaps the child only wants to prolong a delightful situation as much as possible, to continue to have the mother next to the bed, or to sit with her in her easy chair. She should be as comfortable as possible, so she won't want to get up and leave all too soon. . . .

While the fairy tale flows tranquilly between the two, the child can finally enjoy the mother at his ease, observe her face with all its particularities, study the eyes, the mouth, the skin. . . . He certainly listens to the tale, but he permits his attention occasionally to wander as he listens. For example, sometimes he already knows the fairy tale—and for this reason, perhaps, he has cleverly asked for the repetition of a tale he knows—and he needs only to check whether the tale follows the usual plot. In the meantime, his principal occupation can be examining his mother's face, or the face of the adult he rarely succeeds in looking at as long as he would like.

The mother's voice does not only speak to him about Little Red Riding Hood or Little Tom Thumb. The voice speaks to him about herself. A semiotician would say that the child, in this case, is interested not only in the *contents* and its *forms*, not only in the *forms of expression*, but in the substance of the expression—that is, in the maternal voice, in its delicate tones, the volume, the modulations, the music that communicates tenderness, that unravels the knots of anxiety, and makes the ghosts of fear vanish.

Right afterward—or rather, at the same time—contact with the mother tongue is established, with its words, its forms, its structure. We can never mark the exact moment in which children, while listening to a fairy tale, appropriate this language by absorbing a certain relationship between the terms of the discourse, discover how to use verbs, or how prepositions function, but it seems certain to me that the fairy tale gives children an abundant supply of information about the language. Their effort to understand the fairy tale forms part of their effort to understand the words that constitute it; to establish analogies between these words; to carry out deductions; to enlarge or restrict the field of references, the boundaries of a synonym, the sphere of influence of an adjective; and to make them more precise or to correct them. In this "decodification," such linguistic activity is not an additional aspect, but is just as determining as the others. And I am speaking about "activity" in order to emphasize how children take elements from the fairy tale, from the situation, and from all the events of reality—that is, those elements that interest the children and those that place them in a continual process of choosing.

In what other ways does the fairy tale help the child? It helps structure his or her consciousness and establish relationships between "me and the others," "me and the things," "invented and genuine things." It also helps the child to realize distance in space ("far/near") and in time ("one time/now," "before/after," "yesterday/today/tomorrow"). The "once upon a time" of the fairy tale is not different from the "once upon a time" of history, even if the reality of the fairy tale—as the child discovers very quickly—is different from the reality in which he or she lives.

I remember a conversation that I had with a three-year-old girl who asked me, "And then, what shall I do then?"

"Then, you'll go to school."

"And after that?"

"And after that, to another school where you'll learn more things."

"And after that again?"

"When you get big, you'll get married. . . ."

"Not on your life."

"Why not?"

"*Because I don't live in a fairy tale world, I live in the real world.*"

To marry was for her a verb from fairy tales, the final verb, the destiny of the princess and her prince, in a world that was not hers.

From this viewpoint, the fairy tale represents a useful initiation into humanity—into the world of human destinies, as Italo Calvino wrote in his preface to *Italian Folktales*, to the world of history.

It has been said, and it is true, that fairy tales offer a rich repertoire of characters and destinies in which the child finds clues of reality that he or she still does not know, and clues of the future about which he or she still does not think. It has also been said, and this too is true, that fairy tales reflect cultural models that are for the most part archaic and anachronistic, in contrast to the social and technological reality that the child will encounter as he or she grows up. The objection to fairy tales by certain parents and educators collapses, however, if we consider that fairy tales constitute a separate world for the child, a puppet theater from which we adults are separated by a thick curtain. Fairy tales are not objects of imitation but of contemplation. And contemplation has an activating impact, compelling the interests of the listeners to take precedence over the contents of the fairy tale. In addition, when the child reaches the "realistic" phase of childhood, the period when content becomes critical, fairy tales lose their interest for the child, exactly because their "forms" no longer provide raw material for the child's actions.

One senses that children both contemplate and create the structures of their own imaginations at the same time, constructing an indispensable instrument for getting to know reality and mastering it.

Listening is training. For children fairy tales have the same seriousness and truthfulness as a game: they help them learn to become involved, to know themselves, to measure themselves. For example, to measure themselves against fear. All that is said about the negative effects that "scary and violent" fairy tales can have on children—the monstrous creatures, the fearful witches, blood and death (Little Tom Thumb cuts off the heads of the seven daughters of the ogre)—does not seem convincing to me. Everything depends on the conditions under which the child encounters the wolf, in a manner of speaking. If it is the mother's voice he hears, in the peace and security of the family situation, the child can overcome these challenges without fear. The child can pretend to be afraid (a game that has its significance in the formation of defense mechanisms), because he is certain that the father's strength and the mother's courage would be enough to drive off the wolf.

"If you had been there, you would have chased away the wolf, right?"

"Of course, and I would have given him a good beating."

On the other hand, if the child is overcome by fear and cannot do anything about it, we would have to conclude that the fear had already been in him before the wolf entered the story: it was in him, deep within him where he was conflict-ridden. The wolf is then a *symptom* that reveals the fear. It does not *cause* it. . . .

If it is the mother who tells the story of Little Tom Thumb abandoned in the forest with his brothers, the child does not fear that he himself will have the same sort of misfortunes, and can focus his entire attention on the remarkable cunning of the tiny hero. If the mother is away, if the parents are away, and if someone else tells the same story, this person can truly frighten the child—but only because the storyteller reveals to the child the child's condition of "abandonment." And if the mother were not to return? Here we have the reason for his sudden fear. Here we have projected the shadow of unconscious fears, of the experience of loneliness, onto the "axis of listening"—the memory of the time when the child awoke and cried out a few times, and nobody answered him. The decodification does not occur according to laws that are the same for everyone, but according to private laws that are highly personal. One can talk about a "typical listener" only in very broad terms. In fact, no reader is exactly like another.

36 • The Child Who Reads Comics

IF THERE IS an "axis of listening," there is also an "axis of reading." It can lead to interesting discoveries if we explore, follow, and imagine the mental process of a child reading a comic book.

The child is six or seven years old. He has passed through the phase in which his father read the comics aloud to him, or when he invented his own way of reading by interpreting the scenes by clues noted only by him. Now he knows how to read. The comic book is his first really spontaneous reading material. Self-motivated, he reads because he wants to know what happens and not because it is a homework assignment. He reads for himself, not for others (the teacher), not to make a good impression (high marks).

At first, he must distinguish and recognize the characters in the situations that follow one another, and be able to recall their identities in the different positions and the changing expressions they assume. As they are depicted in various colors, he must interpret their meaning: red, anger; yellow, fear. . . . But the code of the "psychological color" is not given only once; it can be recreated each time by the artist. The code can be rediscovered and reconstructed time and again.

The child must attribute a voice to the characters. It is true that in nearly every balloon the point of departure is indicated with precision: it is the mouth when the character speaks; it is the head when the character thinks (and there are other significant distinctions to be made between the way thoughts and words are presented).

When the characters speak with one another, the child must attribute the sentences to one or another. He or she must grasp the sequence in which they are being spoken. (In comic books, time does not always go from left to right like the typographical line.) The child must grasp whether the words are spoken simultaneously, whether one character is speaking and another is thinking, whether one of them is thinking one thing and saying another, et cetera.

At the same time, the child must recognize and distinguish the surroundings, external and internal; note their modifications, their influence on the characters; and comprehend the elements that anticipate what can happen to a character if the character does a certain thing or goes to a certain place without knowing why, for this character is not omniscient like the attentive reader. In the comic book, the surroundings are rarely decorative; they are functional to the narrative and its structure.

An active intervention—indeed, a highly active intervention of the imagination—is required to fill the spaces between one box and the next. At the movies, or in front of a television screen, the images follow each other continuously, describing the action and plot point by point. In the comic book, the action can begin in the first frame and end in the very next one, skipping over all the intermediate passages. The character of the first frame can be riding boldly on his horse, and in the second he can be lying in the dust on the ground: the fall is to be imagined. The final effect is visible from a certain gesture, but not the development. The objects present themselves in a changed order: it is necessary to imagine the course of action that each one takes from the original order to the next. All this work is entrusted to the reader's mind. While a movie is a script, the comic book is stenography from which the reader must reconstruct the text.

In the meantime, the reader must not lose sight of the indicated sounds in each one of the panels, and grasp the nuances (a "squash" is not a "screech") and distinguish the cause. In the more banal comic books, the alphabet of the noises is very limited and coarse. In the funny ones, or in the more sophisticated comics, the elementary noises are often complemented by innovations that must also be deciphered.

The entire course of the story must be reconstructed in the imagination, combining the captions, dialogue, and noise with the drawing and the color so that all the loose strings of the plot that constitute the scenario and the intricate passages can be tied together in a comprehensive manner and made into one. And it is the reader who gives sense to everything: to the characters who are not described, but shown in action; to their relations that result from the action and its developments; to the action that reveals itself to the reader only through gaps and fragments.

For a child of six or seven years of age, comic books seem to me to be sufficiently demanding, rich with logical and imaginative operations—the value of their content aside, for this is not the issue here. The imagination of the child does not remain inactive; rather it is solicited to take a position, to analyze and synthesize, to classify and decide. There is no room here for empty fantasizing, as long as the mind is compelled to pay close attention to complex matters and the imagination is called upon to perform its most noble functions.

I would say that up to a certain point the child's principal interest in comic books is not determined by their contents, but is tied directly to the form and substance of the comics themselves. Children want to master the means of reading the comics. That's it. *They read comic books in order to learn how to read comic books,* to grasp their rules and conventions. They enjoy the efforts of their own imaginations more than the adventures of the characters. They play with their own minds, not with the story. It may be that the things cannot be so clearly separated like this. But it is worth the effort to distinguish them if the distinction helps us not to underestimate children, especially not in this case—not to underestimate their basic seriousness, the moral engagement that they bring to everything they do.

Everything else about comics has already been said, good and bad, and I shall not repeat it.

37 · The Goat of Signor Séguin

ONE TIME IN CLASS the pupils of Mario Lodi read Alphonse Daudet's story about the poor little goat of Signor Séguin. This goat became tired of the rope that his owner had tied around its neck, and fled to the mountains, where the wolf—after a heroic struggle—ate the little goat. I saved the old number of *Insieme* (*Together*), the class newspaper, which the pupils of Vho, the small town in Italy where Lodi teaches, publish year after year, one generation after the next, and send to their friends. Here is the discussion that followed the reading by the class, which they printed in *Insieme*:

> WALTER: Daudet wrote the story about a goat, the goat of Signor Séguin, and we discussed it because we didn't agree with him.
>
> ELVINA: Daudet's goat fled because it wanted to be free, and the wolf ate it. We reworked the story in another way.
>
> FRANCESCA: The master [*padrone*] told the goat that there was a wolf in the mountains, but he told this to the goat because he wanted to keep it prisoner to get its milk.
>
> DANILA: We wrote that the goat fled and found happiness as soon as it was free in the mountains.
>
> MIRIAM: Just like humans want to live in freedom, so does our goat want to live in freedom.
>
> MARIO: It had a right to live that way. If the wolf had come, all the goats together could have killed it with their horns.
>
> MIRIAM: I think that Daudet wanted to teach us that if you disobey, you get into trouble.

WALTER: But our goat, who jumped over a fence, disobeyed its master who kept it prisoner to steal its milk. So it was not a case of disobedience. The goat was rebelling against a thief.

MARIO: Exactly. Because the man robbed milk from the goat who just wanted to be free.

MIRIAM: But he needed the goat's milk.

FRANCESCA: But all goats need freedom. The master could have led the goat to graze in the mountain, and the goat would have given him the milk.

WALTER: But, as Daudet said, the goat did not want a rope around its neck any longer. It didn't want a rope, long *or* short!

FRANCESCA: This story made me think about the struggle of the Italians who liberated themselves from the Austrians.

MIRIAM: When the Italians were free, they were happy like the goat when it arrived in the mountains.

At this point in the newspaper, the text of the children's rewritten story was printed. It concerns the dream of the little goat that is fulfilled by the victory of free goats living together on free mountains.

I have chosen this text in order to follow, in another direction, the axis of reading that began with the child who reads comic books. It is also a perfect example of what the theoreticians of information mean when they maintain that "the decoding of a message always happens according to the code of the receiver."

In reality, Daudet's story lends itself to more subtle interpretations. It is not simply a case of a disobedient act that is punished. In the end, the goat heroically accepts death in battle. One could appropriately end it with the motto: "Better to die than to live in chains." But the children of Vho, who refused to get involved in ambiguous nuances—as the ways of humor are often ambiguous—were quick to see a reactionary moral in the story, which they immediately attacked. They were not convinced that the tragic end of the goat was glorious. For them, the hero had to win. Justice had to triumph.

The children all focused on the story's contents, and they paid no attention to Daudet's elegant language. In the course of their discussion, they do, however, present different viewpoints.

Miriam does not seem at all inclined to negate the warning that "when you disobey, you get into trouble," and with a female capacity to put herself in the situation of others, she recognizes that the man "needs the goat's milk."

Francesca is content with a reformist compromise: "The man could take the goat to graze in the mountains and it would have given milk to him."

Walter is the most consequent and the most radical: "The goat did not want a rope, whether long or short."

In the end, the collective's system of values has its way with its key words *freedom, right,* and *unity* ("Strength through Solidarity").

The children of Vho have lived and worked for years in a small democratic community that requires and stimulates their creative participation instead of repressing it, shunting it, or instrumentalizing it. This can be seen in the two extraordinary books by Mario Lodi, *C'è speranza se questo accade al Vho* (*There Is Hope If It Happens in Vho*) and *Il paese sbagliato* (*The Mistaken Country*). These books explain how the children feel full of hope when they pronounce words like *liberty, right,* and *unity.* They are not words that are simply learned, but rather they are experienced and mastered. The children enjoy their freedom of speech and their freedom of expression. They are accustomed to criticizing any kind of material, including the printed word. They do not know anything about test questions and grades. Each moment of their work is a vital act, independent from bureaucratic programs, didactic routines, and school regulations. It is a moment of life, not an academic moment.

This is why the discussion of Daudet's story was not an academic exercise for them, but a necessity.

The students in Vho are mostly children of farm laborers, and we are in a small farmhouse of the Po Valley, in a region that has a strong tradition of social and political struggle, that contributed a great deal to the Resistance during World War II. The word *master* (*padrone*) has a precise meaning for the children. It has the face of the *padrone* of the farm. It is the face of the owner-enemy. And it is essentially the word *padrone* that determines how the decoding of the message takes place in their imaginations.

When Francesca and Miriam join the consensus of the collective interpretation, they depart from the basis of class struggle, remembering the "struggle of the Italians to liberate themselves from the Austrians." That is, they recall vague mythological figures from their schoolbooks. But the decisive comparison had already been articulated emphatically by Walter, when he equated the *padrone* with a thief. On the basis of this equation, the distinction between disobedience and rebellion is made possible.

Francesca had spoken about the *padrone* who kept the goat prisoner to "get" its milk. But Walter energetically rejected the verb *to get* and its academic overtones ("wool *is gotten* from sheep . . .") in order to change it unequivocally into a violent *to steal.* Thus, in the discussion, the words of the written text lose their weight, and other words take their place to reshape the story in an independent way.

The Roman classical writers already said: "de te fabula narratur" ("the story is told by you"). Even children who do not know Latin tell themselves the stories that they hear. The children of Vho practically forgot the goat and placed themselves and the *padrone* in its place—their fathers who are farm laborers, and the present-day *padrone*.

In the imagination of the young reader (like the young listener), the message does not engrave itself like a sharp graver in wax, but rather collides with all the force of the child's personality. This becomes very clear in the example of Mario Lodi's pupils, who were inclined to make the self-reflective aspect of the written story more explicit, and to express themselves in a creative way. However, there is always a conflict. It can take place in the subconscious and remain unproductive, if the children are conditioned merely to listen in order to conform to what they have heard, and to read within the limits of the cultural and ethical models imposed by the text. But in most such cases children only pretend to do what their education demands. . . .

If you tell the story of Signor Séguin's goat to children, emphasizing the apologetic aspect of the narrative and the "trouble" that children would have if they are disobedient, they will understand that you expect them to condemn disobedience severely. They will also give you a written report if you require it. They will even succeed in convincing themselves superficially that they believe what they have written. But it will not be true. They will have lied to you just as children lie every day when they write in their compositions exactly what they believe grown-ups want to read. As far as they are concerned, the children will be content to forget the story about the goat as soon as they can, just as they forget the other moralistic stories. . . .

The decisive encounter between children and books happens in the classrooms of schools. If it happens in a creative situation, where life counts and not the exercise, a certain pleasure in reading can arise from it, a pleasure with which one is not born, because it is not an instinct. If the encounter happens in a bureaucratic situation, if the book is "humiliated" by being made into an instrument for exercises (copying, summary of the contents, grammatical exercises, et cetera), if it is suffocated by the traditional academic routines (questions about the story and graded papers), the *technique* of reading can be developed, but not the *pleasure*. The children will learn how to read, but they will read only out of a sense of obligation. They will take refuge in comic books—even when they are capable of reading more complex and richer material—perhaps only because the comic books have not been contaminated by school.

38 • Stories for Playing

I TELL A GROUP OF CHILDREN a ghost story from the radio program *Tante storie per giocare* (*Many Stories for Playing*). The ghosts live on Mars. Actually, they have a miserable existence because nobody takes them seriously. They are mocked by children and grown-ups alike, and they no longer have fun rattling old rusty chains. . . . Finally, they decide to emigrate to Earth where, according to their sources of information, many people are still afraid of ghosts.

The children laugh and swear that they are not afraid of ghosts.

"The story stops here," I say. "We have to continue and finish it. What do you propose?"

Here are the answers:

"While they are on their way to Earth, someone changes the signposts in space, and the ghosts land on a distant planet."

"It is not necessary to change the signposts. The ghosts can't see because they have sheets over their eyes. They miss the right path and land on the moon."

"A few of them arrive on Earth, but there are too few of them to scare the people."

Five children between the ages of six and nine, who a moment before had agreed that ghosts were ridiculous, are now very much in agreement that the ghosts should be stopped from invading Earth. As listeners they felt secure enough to laugh. On the other hand, as narrators, they obeyed an inner voice that recommended caution. Their imagination is now directed by an unconscious reference to all their fears (ghosts and, of course, other things that might be represented by ghosts).

Thus the children's impulses and feelings have an influence on the mathematics of the imagination. The story can proceed only through multiple filters. Even represented openly as a grotesque story, it was felt as a threat. The "code of the receiver" tripped an alarm where the "code of the sender" had intended to cause laughter.

At this point, the narrator can choose between a reassuring ending ("the ghosts end up at the bottom of the Milky Way") or a provocative ending ("they land on Earth where they cause all kinds of mischief"). At that time I myself chose a surprise ending: in the vicinity of the moon, the ghosts who have fled Mars meet some ghosts who have fled Earth for the same reason. Together they sink into the abyss of the universe. Here I tried to balance the fear with a "laugh of superiority." If I made a mistake, I shall repent.

To another group of children who took part in the same radio program, I proposed the story about a man who cannot sleep because he hears moans and groans each night. He does not find peace and quiet until he has helped everyone near and far who needs him. (In the story he can move from one spot of the Earth to another in a matter of seconds). A simple parable about solidarity. However, as we began talking about a possible ending, the first child I asked for a suggestion said without hesitation, "Well, I would have stuffed my ears with cotton!"

If we were to deduce from this answer that the concerned child was an egotist and asocial, that would be easy but off-target. All children are naturally egocentric. In reality, the child had "decoded" the comic side of the situation, giving it more weight than the emotional side: he did not listen to the moans and groans, but he placed himself in the situation of a poor man who was not allowed to sleep in peace night after night, no matter what the reason was.

I want to add that we were in Rome and that the Romans, even the children, are quick to make witty remarks. Moreover, these children were particularly uninhibited—they were in a recording studio and had already been there a few times—and they were accustomed to say the first thing that came into their heads. Finally, there is juvenile exhibitionism that one must take into account.

Later in the discussion the same boy was one of the first to recognize that the world is full of suffering, visible or hidden, full of bad things, and that whoever truly feels that he should do something about suffering wherever it occurs does not have much time to sleep. But his first reaction was equally significant; it suggests to me that the story about this man, too full of good intentions, needs to find an ending more adventurous than sentimental. He must be positioned so he can triumph over his enemies rather than continue to suffer. (In fact, at that time the story ended this way: the man who left his home to help others each night is mistaken for a thief and put in prison. But the people whom he had helped all over the world come running and free him.)

It is impossible to predict which detail in the story, which word, which passage will determine the "decoding."

Another time I told the story of a Pinocchio who becomes rich by accumulating and selling the wood he acquires through his lies. With each lie, his nose becomes longer. Once I opened the discussion about the ending, all the children imagined a conclusion in which this Pinocchio is punished. The equation "lie = bad" is part of a system of values that needs no discussion. Moreover, this Pinocchio was identified as a swindler, and justice demands that the swindler be punished in the end. In short, the children punished the cunning Pinocchio, even if they were amused by his story, because they were doing their duty. None of them had enough worldly experience to know that a certain type of thief, far from ending up in prison, can become a first-class citizen and a pillar of society; the children did not come up with the ending in which Pinocchio becomes the richest and most famous man in the world and has a monument built in his honor during his lifetime.

The discussion becomes more lively and creative when it centers on finding the appropriate type of punishment. Here the obligatory pair "lie/truth" assumes its function. The children decide that the entire wealth of the swindler will go up in smoke right at the very moment that he tells the truth. However, since Pinocchio is cunning and is always on guard not to tell the truth, it is necessary to find a trick to make him tell it despite himself. The search for this trick becomes very amusing. The same "truth"—that one accepts as a value but is not amusing—becomes amusing the very moment spice is added through the "trick."

At this point, the children no longer play the part of the judge who must avenge the damaged truth, but the part of a swindler who must at all costs dupe another swindler. The conventional morality is only an alibi for their entertainment, which frankly is amoral. It seems to be a law: there is no authentic creation without a certain ambiguity.

Open stories—that is, the unfinished ones and those with different possible endings—assume the form of an imaginative problem: one has certain data at one's disposal, and one must decide if their combination will lead to a solution. There are various kinds of calculations that enter into this decision: fantastical ones, based on the pure movement of the images; moral ones, related to content; sentimental ones, related to experience; and ideological ones, if a "message" rises to the surface and calls for clarification. It can happen that one begins to discuss the ending of the story and discovers instead a theme that has nothing to do with the story. In my opinion, one must feel free at this point to abandon the story to its fate and to accept the coincidental suggestion.

39 • When Grandfather Becomes a Cat

MANY TIMES I have told an unfinished story about a retired old man to various groups of children in Italy and other countries. This man feels that he is useless at home because everyone, adults and children, is too preoccupied to pay attention to him. Therefore, he decides to go live with the cats.

No sooner said than done. He goes to the Piazza dell'Argentina (we are in Rome), ducks under the iron bar that divides the street from the archeological zone (the realm of the stray cats), and all at once he is transformed into a handsome gray cat. After he has various adventures, he returns to his home. But he returns as a cat. And as a cat he is accepted and welcomed. The comfortable easy chair is there for him. He is petted and given milk and pieces of meat. As a grandfather he was a nobody. As a cat he is the center of attention in the home. . . .

At this point I ask the children: "Would you like the grandfather to remain a cat or to return to his human form as grandfather?"

Ninety-nine times out of a hundred the children prefer that the cat become the grandfather again, for the sake of justice and out of empathy, or perhaps to free themselves from an unpleasant inquietude that can engender a feeling of guilt. They want the grandfather to be recuperated, reintegrated with all his human rights, and reconciled. That is the rule.

Until now I have encountered only two exceptions. One time a boy insisted emphatically that it would be better for the grandfather if he remained a cat forever in order to punish those who had offended him. And a five-year-old girl, a little pessimist, said: "He should remain a cat. Otherwise everything will begin all over again, and nobody will want to pay attention to him."

The meaning of these two exceptions is fully clear. Both are also marked by sympathy for the grandfather.

I follow my first question right away with another question: "But what must the cat do to become the grandfather again?"

The children, no matter where I have told this story, north or south, do not hesitate to propose the solution: "He must duck under the bar, but go in the opposite direction."

The bar is made into the magical instrument of transformation. When I told the story for the first time, it did not occur to me at all. The children revealed this to me and taught me this rule: "Whoever ducks beneath the bar and goes one way becomes a cat; whoever goes the opposite way becomes human again."

With the bar as the means of separation, however, it would also be possible to distinguish between "going beneath" and "going over." But nobody has ever proposed this to me. It is apparent that the ritual use of the bar must respect very precise rules, and the variations cannot be exaggerated. If you "go over the bar," this is reserved for cats that come and go and remain cats. . . . And, in fact, a child raised this point one time by saying, "Why is it that the cat, when he ducks under the bar to return home, doesn't become the grandfather right away?" Then another child was quick to answer, "But he didn't crawl under the bar this time, he went over it. He climbed over the bar."

Now, after all this, we are left with the sneaking suspicion that the re-transformation of the cat into the grandfather is not always determined exclusively by motives of justice, but also by reasons of symmetry in the imagination. A magical occurrence had taken place in one direction, and the imagination, without knowing it, waited for it to happen in the magical opposite direction.

If a reader is to have complete satisfaction, there must be a logical-formal aspect to a story that accompanies the moral aspect. Here the solution was produced by the mathematical mind and the heart together.

If at times one has the impression that only the heart decides, then this is due to a defective analysis. When I say this, I naturally do not want to deny the fact that the heart has its "reasons" in the sense indicated by Pascal. But the imagination, too, has its reasons, as we have seen.

40 • Games in the Pine Forest

10:30 A.M. George (age seven) and Roberta (age five and a half) leave the hotel and head toward the surrounding pine forest.

ROBERTA: "Do you want to go look for lizards?"

I, who am observing all this from a window, understand perfectly well why she has made this proposal. Roberta grabs the lizards with her hands. In contrast, George is disgusted by this. Generally, George proposes that they have a race because he is faster. On the other hand, Roberta would rather draw because she can do it better. Nature is unfair in its innocence.

They set out slowly. Then they start looking for lizards, but they are really looking for chance. This is also what Novalis says: "Playing is experimenting with chance." They avoid large spaces and stay near the kitchen at the back of the hotel where the pine forest is more familiar to them. They arrive at a pile of firewood.

ROBERTA: "Let's hide here now."

The present "now" is the signal that the waiting is over. The "feeling around" has now taken the form of a game. The word *now* stabilizes the distance between the world as it is and the world transformed into symbols of a game to be played. They circle the pile of firewood slowly, and they take out a few pieces of wood.

They are regular pieces of wood, manageable, sawed-off pieces for the kitchen, and the two begin to carry them away. Behind the pile of firewood there is a box and a large basket. They fetch them. Now George takes over and leads the game.

GEORGE: "We're in the jungle, hunting tigers."

The pine forest that forms part of the daily reality of the vacation does not interest them as such: here it is reduced or promoted to a "sign" with a new meaning. "When things become signs," says Dewey, "and acquire the representative capacity to replace other things, the game is transformed from pure physical exuberance into an activity that includes a mental aspect."

They change their spot and move toward a large rock that emerges from the ground. The basket and the box become two huts. (They continue to assign new roles to the objects.) They collect little sticks for the fireside. The game takes the form here of an open system. It proceeds by discovering and inventing analogies. The word *jungle* suggested the word *hut*. But now their experience intervenes: the children have played this sort of game many times at home, and they insert that game into the jungle game.

ROBERTA: "Let's make a fire."

GEORGE: "Time to go to bed."

Each one retires into a "hut." They lay down there for a few seconds.

ROBERTA: "Now it's morning, and I've got to look for chickens to keep in our chicken coop."

GEORGE: "No, the chickens have to be cooked for lunch."

They run about and collect pine cones. It is 11:15.

Here it is important to note that a day has passed in the game. The time of the game is not real time, but more of an exercise with time, a recapitulation of the experience of time: it is evening, one goes to bed; it is morning, one gets up. Collecting pine cones in a pine forest would have been the easiest activity at the beginning. Instead, the pine cones were neglected until the moment that the children took them from their botanical context and gave them the function of "chickens," endowing them with a new meaning.

11:20 A.M. Only five minutes have passed since they "slept," and yet they return to their huts to "sleep" again.

A new intrusion: the other classical "father-mother game" is projected onto the axis of the jungle game. In part, this is the unconscious meaning of the "going to sleep."

GEORGE: "I want to hear silence."

George makes this remark with a particular intonation—it is probably that of his teacher when she orders the children to be quiet at school. Note the continual fluctuation between the level of experience and the level of invention.

ROBERTA: "Cock-a-doodle-do! Time to get up."

Spurred by George's dramatization of "playing the teacher," the girl responds by "playing the rooster." With the two remarks, the children have transformed themselves into "signs," George into the teacher, Roberta into the rooster. And a second day has passed. Why all this time? Perhaps to augment the distance between the game, the creation, and the world of habits. To be "further away" . . . "more into" the game.

GEORGE: "Now it's off to the hunt!"

They get up, wander in silence for a while. Then they return to the pile of firewood.

11:23 A.M.

ROBERTA: "I'm drinking a beer."

GEORGE: "I'm drinking an apéritif."

The pile of firewood has provisionally become a bar. It is not clear why this deviation has taken place in the game. Perhaps they have exhausted its subject. But it is more probable that, since they ate their breakfast in haste, they feel hungry and want to eat something, at least symbolically. As hunters they obviously have the right to drink things that are normally forbidden.

George has a belt with two pistols. He takes one out of its holster and offers it to Roberta. At the beginning of the game he had not thought of doing this, and Roberta was too proud to ask him for one. Now, after they have been asleep two times, the offer has the meaning of a declaration: George declares to Roberta that they are equals in the game. But only this?

ROBERTA (pointing the pistol toward her head): "I'm going to commit suicide."

All this happens in a few seconds, as in a flashing dramatic scene of love. We would truly need to hear what a psychologist has to say about this scene.

ROBERTA: "I'm a mummy now, and you run away."

As far as I can tell, the mummy has been taken from TV.

11:25 A.M. They bring back the wood to the pile of firewood as if they had finished playing their game. George is the type of boy who has been taught "to return things to their place." In the new work a rhythm is suddenly visible: George collects the wood, and Roberta throws it onto the pile.

ROBERTA: "I've thrown it all." This use of the past perfect indicates that the action of collecting and returning the pieces of wood to the pile has itself been transformed into a game, into a "sign" of itself. "I'm throwing the wood" means work, fatigue. "I've thrown it all" is the assumption of a role.

11:35 A.M. Near the pile of firewood there is a scale. The children begin to play at weighing themselves. But they do not succeed. George's grandmother intervenes as an "expert." Then she goes away.

11:40 A.M. Roberta sits down in the cardboard box and proposes they play clowns. She pretends to fall and rolls herself on the ground. George does not accept her idea and says instead: "Let's go sliding."

They fetch the box and bring it to the large rock where they create a simple "slide." Then they slide down several times.

11:43 A.M. The slide has become a boat. Both of them sit in it. They row between the pile of firewood and the rock.

GEORGE: "Here's the island. Let's get out. We've got to tie up the boat. Otherwise, it will float away."

They climb onto the rock.

There is a new transformation of things in the works. First the rock has become an island, and now the pine forest is no longer a jungle but a sea.

They fetch the basket again so that each one of them has a boat.

11:50 A.M. They sail toward the scale, which has become another island.

ROBERTA: "It's now the next day."

This time they have not "slept" to pass from one day to the next. It is sufficient just to state it. In reality the new leap in time is meant to underscore the distance between the jungle game and the sea game. As they drag the boats behind them, they sing. Then they get into them and begin to sail again. George's box turns over. Roberta: "There's a storm at sea." George's fall is not intentional. The present tense immediately utilizes the mistake in a creative way, interpreting it within the logic of the game.

George turns his box over several times. Since he wants to cover up his clumsiness, he repeats his mistake in a clown-like show. Roberta laughs. George is now "acting the clown." Roberta's laughter is ample compensation for him. Is there an element of courting in this show, of the "wedding dance"?

GEORGE: "Land! Land!"

ROBERTA: "Hurray!"

They land near a pine tree.

GEORGE: "Peace and prosperity!"

George lives in a region where he frequently encounters Franciscan monks, who ask for alms. Perhaps he has also played at being a monk sometimes. It is not possible to reconstruct the origins of this new insertion. When monks enter a house, they use this form of greeting ("Peace and prosperity"). The arrival near the pine tree must have been for George a kind of arrival at home. In the game, as in the dream, the imagination condenses images at a rapid pace. Note also that the appearance of the "islands" explains the initial sentences of the morning in a consequential manner: "Let's hide here." The children are now really "hidden," far from everything, surrounded everywhere by the sea.

11:57 A.M. George becomes aware that they have lost the pistols. They do not know where to look for them. The preceding minute has sunk for them deeply into a past that they do not know how to reconstruct. From the window I point to the pistols, and they go to fetch them without wondering how I know everything.

12 noon. They exchange boats. Now Roberta has the box. She turns it over. One of the sides opens like a door. The association is so inviting that the boat becomes a house again. Now they go hunting for rabbits.

The "rabbits" are the same pine cones that had been "chickens" before this. They are never pine cones during their play.

12:05 P.M. They have collected the pine cones in the box.

ROBERTA: "I'll stay here in my little house forever."

GEORGE: "I'm going to rest."

The future and the continuing present tenses of the two verbs designate the distance to the game: a kind of intermission for resting.

When they resume playing, it seems that the game has taken two directions. George shoots at some rabbits, and Roberta must go and pick them up, while at the same time she searches for other things for her "little villa."

ROBERTA: "I'm raising chickens."

GEORGE (who has returned to the basket to sail in his boat): "I'm coming to visit you because we're friends."

For a few minutes more the game wavers and peters out. George decides to stop, by sitting on the swing and calling Roberta to come and push him. With very few interruptions, the swing keeps them busy until lunchtime.

All that I have hinted at here—just as one can indicate a motif on an instrument without really playing it—is a "reading" of the game as if it were a "story in action." I am not a stenographer. At the time I observed these authentic games (approximately ten years ago), I did not own a tape recorder, and I could only write down my observations in a notebook. I should have discussed these notes with a psychologist, et cetera, et cetera.

But for the purpose of the present micro-grammar of the imagination, the preceding pages should be sufficient to suggest how the contributions and solicitations of the "axes," which we investigated in the analysis of the story "Peter and the Putty," converge just like they do on the "axis of the game" and in a free text—the axis of the verbal selection, the axis of the experience, the axis of the unconscious (the short and terrible game with the pistols . . .), the axis that introduces values into the game ("the order" in which George places the pieces of wood back onto the pile).

To explain a game fully, one would have to be able to reconstruct step by step how the symbolization of the objects occurs, how the modifications and changes and the "fluctuation of meaning" come about. Although psychology is certainly valuable in such an undertaking, it is insufficient. It is not psychology but rather linguistics or semiotics that can explain how the action of throwing the wood onto the pile of firewood, experienced in the present tense, requires a verb in the past perfect tense; and how certain analogies between the objects of a game impose themselves sometimes through form and sometimes through meaning.

We have many intelligent theories about play, but we still do not have a phenomenology of the imagination, which gives life to play.

41 • Imagination, Creativity, School

THE ENTRY on *intuition* in the *Encyclopaedia Britannica* includes Kant, Spinoza, and Bergson, but not Benedetto Croce. To be sure, it is not exactly the same thing as talking about relativity without mentioning Einstein, but it is close. Poor Benedetto. I have such great sympathy for him that I have arbitrarily placed my discovery at the beginning of this chapter. And I hope that, with this simple procedure, I have acquired the right to shape the following chapter as unsystematically and unpretentiously as possible.

From the supply of the philosophical dictionaries and encyclopedias I have at hand in my home and at my office, I note first of all that for a long time the terms *imagination* and *fantasy* have been considered as belonging exclusively to the history of philosophy. Psychology, which is still relatively young, began occupying itself with these terms only a few decades ago. Consequently, it is not astonishing that *imagination*, in our schools, is still treated like a poor relative in comparison with *attention* and *memory*. To listen patiently and to remember scrupulously always constitute the characteristics of the model student, who is generally the most accommodating and most malleable.

The classical writers, from Aristotle to Saint Augustine, did not have two different words in their language to distinguish between imagination and fantasy and to assign them different functions. Nor did it occur to Bacon or Descartes, with all their clear thinking, to do so. It is only in the eighteenth century, with Christian Wolff, that we have the first distinction between the faculty to perceive sensual things that are not present and the *facultas fingendi* (creative capability), which consists in "producing the image of a thing never perceived by the senses through the separation and composition of the images." In this regard, my standard history of philosophy tells me that Kant elaborated catalogues of "reproductive imagination" and "productive imagination," and Fichte attributed a greater effect to the latter over the former.

But it is to Hegel that we owe the creation of the definitive distinction between imagination and fantasy. For him both were determinants of intelligence: but intelligence as imagination was simply reproductive, while as fantasy it was creative. Clearly and hierarchically separated, the two terms serve egregiously to sanction a somewhat genetic, almost physiological, distinction between the poet (artist) capable of using creative fantasy and the common man, the mere worker, capable only of using the imagination that serves him for purely practical purposes, like imagining a bed when he is tired, and a dinner table when he is hungry. Fantasy in group A, imagination in group B. . . .

It is up to the philosophers to theorize about accomplished facts. And in this case the accomplished fact is what Marx and Engels identify in *German Ideology*: "The exclusive concentration of talent in some individuals and its suppression in the broad masses are the consequences of the division of labor."

Here we have the pillars of society. And the theory of a qualitative difference between the common man and the (bourgeois) artist forms a perfect fit.

In our present day, neither philosophy nor psychology sees radical differences between imagination and fantasy. It is not considered a mortal sin to use the two terms like synonyms. And we can thank the phenomenologist Edmund Husserl, and also Jean-Paul Sartre, for this. (In Sartre's book, *L'imagination*, there is a wonderful passage that I never tire of repeating: "The imagination is an act, not a thing.")

If there is a distinction to be made, it is between fantasy and fancy (which is addressed by Elémire Zolla in his *Storia del fantasticare*): fantasy constructs with the real and on the real; fancy escapes the real as fast as it can. However, at the same time, 1) Zolla attributes a great part of modern and contemporary art to fancy rather than to fantasy, and therefore, fancy is to be taken in small doses; 2) in *Prelogical Experience*, Edward Tauber and Maurice R. Green demonstrate that even fancy is not to be thrown out like the baby with the bathwater, because it appeals to sources of inner experience that are usually quite inaccessible—a refined informer that can be useful.

A good manual of psychology (I use Gardner Murphy's *An Introduction to Psychology*, which is most helpful) can nowadays provide more information about the imagination than the entire history of philosophy up to Benedetto Croce. After him, there is still Bertrand Russell (*The Analysis of the Mind*) and John Dewey (*How We Think*). One can also benefit from reading L. S. Vygotsky's *The Psychology of Art* and Rudolf Arnheim's *Towards a Psychology of Art*. Naturally, in order to become better acquainted with the world of the child, one should at least read Piaget, Wallon, and Bruner. No matter what you read by these three writers, you cannot go wrong. And if they pull the rug out from under your feet, you can regain your balance with Célestin Freinet.

Unfortunately, Alessandro Manzoni's dialogue *Della invenzione* ("About Invention") is not very fruitful. The title is very promising, but the contents are similar to Antonio Rosmini's work, and there is not a sentence worth remembering.

On the other hand, Vygotsky's book *The Imagination and Creativity of the Child* is a small jewel, which I believe, despite the fact that it is now somewhat old, has two great assets: first, it describes the imagination with clarity and simplicity as a process of the human mind; second, it recognizes that all human beings—and not just a privileged few (the artists) and a select few (determined through tests underwritten by some foundation)—have a common creative capacity. Whatever differences there are between human beings reveal themselves to be produced by social and cultural factors.

The creative function of the imagination belongs to common people, scientists, and technicians. It is just as essential for scientific discoveries as it is for generating works of art. It is absolutely a necessary condition for daily life.

Vygotsky maintains that seeds of the imagination manifest themselves in the games of animals—and even more in the lives of children. The game is not a simple remembrance of impressions, but a creative re-elaboration of them, a process through which children combine the data of experience with other data to construct a new reality corresponding to their curiosity and their needs. But exactly because the imagination constructs only with materials from real life (and therefore the adult can construct to a much greater extent), it is necessary that children be able to grow up in an environment rich in impulses and stimuli to nurture their imaginations, and to apply the imagination to appropriate tasks that reinforce its structures and expand its horizons.

This present grammar of the imagination—it seems to me that here is the place to clarify everything definitively—is not a theory of the child's imagination (this would have to be something else), nor a collection of recipes, nor a textbook of stories but, I believe, a proposal to be placed alongside all the other books that seek to enrich the environment in which the child grows up (at home as well as at school) by providing certain stimuli.

The mind is one solitary thing. Its creativity must be cultivated in all directions. Fairy tales (heard or invented) are not all that can be useful to a child. The liberal use of all the possibilities of language represents just one of the directions in which the child can develop. But *tout se tient*, as the French say. The child's imagination, when stimulated to invent words, will apply the instruments of the imagination in all domains of experience that call for their creative intervention. Fairy tales are useful to mathematics just as mathematics is useful to fairy tales. They are useful for poetry, music, political commitment—in sum, they are useful for everyone, and not just for the dreamer. The real reason they are so useful is because they do not seem to be useful, just like poetry and music, like theater and sports.

They help the complete human being. If a society based on the myth of productivity (and on the reality of profit) needs only half human beings—loyal executors, busy imitators, and docile instruments without a will of their own—that means there is something wrong with this society and it needs to be changed. To change it, creative human beings are needed, people who know how to use their imaginations.

Of course, creative human beings also search for this society, for their own purposes. A. J. Cropley writes candidly in his book *Creativity* that the study of divergent thought must be placed within the framework of "the maximum utilization of all the intellectual resources of the people," and "it is essential for maintaining the proper positions of the world." Many thanks. "Creative people are wanted" because the world should remain as it is. No, Mr. Cropley, instead, let us develop everyone's creativity so that the world will change.

Obviously, it is necessary to know more about this "creativity." After consulting the useful book, *The Creative Imagination* by Théodule Ribot, one can find an illuminating clarification of the concept in *Educazione e creatività* (*Education and Creativity*) by Marta Fattori, in which recent American research is presented, analyzed, and, wherever necessary, criticized. (The

American scholars have produced the first real solid research on this subject; and this is not solely due to the fact that the Americans are richer than other researchers. In many things they are also more attentive and faster. And they know how to do good work.)

"Creativity" is synonymous with "divergent thought," that is, thinking that is capable of continually breaking the schemes of experience. A mind that is always at work is creative, a mind that always asks questions, discovers problems where others find satisfactory answers. It is a mind that prefers fluid situations where others only sense danger, a mind that is capable of making autonomous and independent judgments (also independent from the father, the professor, and the society), that rejects everything that is codified, reshapes objects and concepts without letting itself be hindered by conformist attitudes. All these qualities are manifested in the creative process. And this process—it should be stressed—has a playful character. Always. Even when we are dealing with "strict mathematics." (And here it is necessary to remember that my friend Professor Vittorio Checcucci of the University of Pisa says absolutely the same thing in his book, *Creatività e matematica* [*Creativity and Mathematics*]. He says and demonstrates it with splendid experiments of mathematical games using electronic calculators.)

Also Marta Fattori says in her final analysis that all people can be "creative," provided that they do not live in a repressive society, in a repressive family, attend a repressive school. . . . An education leading to creativity is possible.

The teachers of the Movimento di Cooperazione Educativa reach this conclusion in a publication entitled *La creatività nell'espressione* (*Creativity in Expression*), in which they present some of their research that, it seems to me, was compiled with the implicit motto, "Let us organize a school, that promotes in all the children the cultivation and development of qualities and tendencies that can be pointed to as characteristics of 'creative types.'"

These teachers' achievement seems to me to be particularly important—and it was not accomplished by one person but by a militant movement, the most advanced in the Italian school system. Indeed, when these teachers talk about creativity, they mean the entire curriculum and not just certain subjects. Let me quote:

> In the past, creativity was almost always talked about in reference to the so-called expressive activities and to play, almost in opposition to other experiences, such as the conceptualization of mathematical and scientific terms, the investigation of the environment, historical and geographical research. . . . The fact that even the most committed and well-disposed people relegate the

role of creativity to minor projects is perhaps the best proof that the inhuman system in which we live has the repression of the creative potentiality as one of its main objectives.

Let me quote once more:

Education in mathematics must not be run on the narrow track of technical ability and efficiency, rather it must begin with the recognition that conceptualization is a free and creative function of our minds. . . . Even when we talk about space at schools, it is clear that the fundamental characteristic of a school's space must be its capacity to be transformed. That is, users (children and teachers) must have the possibility to assume an attitude in their encounters with the place that is no longer one of passive acceptance but one of creative active intervention in keeping with their way of life.

To take a step backward (from time to time it can do good to take one or two steps backward), I would like to note that, when using the terms *creative* and *creativity*, one cannot in the least hear the echoes of earlier and more recent attempts—praiseworthy but one-sided—to give the educational activity a sense and a character different from those that the academic institutions had done in conformity with the social role that they accepted.

Schiller—*tanto nomini* (hats off to the great man)—I shall not say more—was the first to speak about an "aesthetic education" (see his letters, *Über die ästhetische Erziehung des Menschen*): "Man only plays when he is a man in the complete sense of the word, and he is only a complete man, when he plays." So wrote the great Schiller. Such a decisive assertion led him straight to the idea of an "aesthetic state," to which he assigned the task "of providing freedom through freedom." It may have been a mistaken idea, but unfortunately we have had instead the "ethical state"—and it has cost blood and tears.

In order to find a parallel idea that is as radical, it is necessary to make a leap of almost two hundred years to Herbert Read and his famous *Education through Art* (1943). Read's major thesis is that artistic activity, and it alone, can realize and develop a kind of comprehensive experience within the child. He perceives that it is not necessary to sacrifice the imagination in order to develop logical thought. On the contrary. And certainly Read's work has had a strong influence in the area of understanding and interpreting children's artwork.

Read's only mistake, to speak *a posteriori*, is that he talked about imagination only in relation to the function of art. Here Dewey saw things better than Read did when he wrote:

The proper function of the imagination is vision of realities and possibilities that cannot be exhibited under existing conditions of sense perception. Clear insight into the remote, the absent, the obscure is its aim. History, literature, and geography, the principles of science, nay, even geometry and arithmetic are full of matters that must be imaginatively realized if they are realized at all. (*How We Think*)

I interrupt the quotation at this point because it is not as interesting after this, and that is a shame.

Creativity in the number one spot. And the teacher?

The teacher—according to the Movimento di Cooperazione Educativa—is transformed into an "animator." Into a promoter of creativity. The teacher no longer transmits beautiful, prepackaged knowledge, a snack a day. The teacher is no longer a circus trainer of ponies and seals. The teacher is an adult who is with the children to express the best in himself or herself, to develop his or her own creative inclination, imagination, and constructive commitment as well, in a series of activities that receive equal consideration. Emotional and moral qualities (the values and norms of living together) are elicited in works of painting, theater, sculpture, and music; one's cognitive ability (natural science, linguistics, sociology) and constructive technology are elicited in games. None of these activities should be treated as mere entertainment or pastimes, in contrast to others that are considered more serious.

There is no hierarchy of fields whatsoever. Basically there is only one field—real life, encountered from all points of view, beginning with the reality of the school community, togetherness, the ways we live and work together. In a school of this kind, the child is no longer a consumer of culture and values, but a creator and producer of values and culture.

These are not just words—they are reflections born out of practical experience in schools, out of a political and cultural struggle, out of many years of commitment and experimentation. They are not recipes; they constitute a new position, a different role. And it is understandable that, at this point, innumerable problems confront these teachers, demanding to be resolved once more. But between a school that is dead and one that is alive there is a true mark of distinction: the school for "consumers" is dead. Pretending to be alive, it cannot avoid putrefaction. A school that is alive and new can only be a school of "creators." This means that there is no such thing as "students" or "teachers," but whole individuals. "A tendency toward an all-around development of the individual," Marx would say (*The Poverty of Philosophy*), "begins to make itself felt."

It is true that he said "begins" and wrote this many years ago. . . . If one sees things in advance, one can be regarded as a dreamer because history's course of time is never identical with that of the individual, and things do not ripen at fixed times like peaches. Marx was not a dreamer, but he had an extremely strong imagination.

And I do not deny that, even today, it takes a great dose of imagination to see beyond the school as it is now, and to imagine the crumbling of its "reformatory with curriculum" walls.

But it also requires that one believe that the world can continue and become more humane. The apocalypse has become fashionable again. The social classes that foresee the decline of their status in the near future perceive this decline in the form of a universal catastrophe, and they read the ecological maps just like the astrologers read the stars in the year 1000.

Old people are egocentric. Giacomo Leopardi, the pessimist with open eyes and sharp mind, fully understood this a long time ago as he copied and commented on a letter, already old at the time, in his notebooks, *Zibaldone*. It was a Sunday in the year 1827, and the letter was already filled with a lament that "the seasons were no longer what they once were."

But you can read it for yourself:

"In the meantime it is certain that the old order of the seasons is gradually becoming mixed up. Here in Italy people have begun talking and quarreling everywhere. Some say that spring and fall no longer exist, and due to the disappearance of clear boundaries there is no doubt that the cold will overcome. I have heard my father say that during his youth in Rome everyone wore summer clothes on Easter Sunday. To whoever does not need to pawn his flannel shirts right now, I recommend that he guard against getting rid of even the smallest thing that he wore in mid-winter." (Magalotti, *Lettere familiari*, Part I, Letter 28, Belmonte, 9 February 1683, a hundred and forty-four years ago!). If those people who maintain that the earth is becoming colder and colder just like the good Doctor Paoli (in his wonderful and scholarly research on the molecular movement of solids), and who have no other evidence to show than the testimony of our old people, who affirm the very same thing that Magalotti says, and allege the same customary thing that they connect with this season, then one can see from this contrast that they would not have much effect with this argument. Magalotti, that old eulogist of the early days of the church, wants to believe that even the natural things in his childhood and youth were better than what came after, because he is dissatisfied with human things. The reason for this is clear, namely, this was the way things seemed to him at that time—the cold did not bother him, he felt it much less, et cetera, et cetera. . . .

With a little practice it is possible to take lessons in optimism even from Giacomo Leopardi.

Notes

Novalis

Novalis, quoted in the first chapter, began to publish his fragments in 1798 when he was twenty-six. In his first collection, entitled *Blütenstaub* (*Pollen*), the following thought occurred to him: "The art of writing books has still not been invented. But it is on the verge of being invented. Fragments of this kind are literary seeds. Of course there may be many unfruitful grains among them—but this doesn't matter as long as some of them flower!" The quote about the fantastic that I cited in this chapter appeared in *Philosophische und andere Fragmente*, and the original reads: "Hätten wir auch eine Phantastik wie eine Logik, so wäre die Erfindungskunst erfunden."

Novalis' *Fragments* shed light everywhere for everyone. For the linguist: "Each person has his own language." For the politician: "Everything practical is economical." For the psychoanalyst: "Sicknesses must be regarded as corporeal insanity and partially like fixed ideas."

Novalis, whose voice was the purest of romanticism, the mystic of "magical idealism," had a knack of perceiving events and problems in reality that his contemporaries were unable to see.

In a good selection of his *Literarische Fragmente* (*Literary Fragments*), there is the following reflection: "Every poetic work interrupts the usual condition, the daily routine of life—similar to what dreams do—in order to reinvigorate us, to keep the very meaning of life itself awake in us."

In order to understand this fragment fully, in my opinion, it is necessary to place it next to another that defines romantic poetry as "the art of making an object strange and nevertheless familiar and attractive."

Read without a code, the two fragments contain perhaps the germ of the "estrangement" of the object, which Victor Shklovsky and the Russian formalists of the 1920s regarded as essential for the artistic process.

"The Word That Plays"

In order to provide some depth to the chapters, "The Stone in the Pond," "The Fantastic Binominal," "The Creative Error," and "Stories for Laughing," in which the "word" was the prime focus, I prepared myself so I could cite the appropriate "literature": a few linguistic studies (Jakobson, Martinet, De Mauro) and many wonderful works on semiotics (Umberto Eco). But I don't want to drop names. That would only, inevitably, reveal my dilettantism, eclecticism, and confusion. I am a simple reader, not a specialist. Like many other people, I discovered ethnography and ethnology through the writer Cesare Pavese, who began editing a famous series of books on these themes for the publisher Einaudi. I discovered linguistics some years after I abandoned the university, where I succeeded—certainly with the university's help—in never having a clue about linguistics. At least I learned one thing. If one has something to do with children and wants to understand what they do and what they say, pedagogy is not sufficient, and psychology is not able fully to represent all their expressions and actions. It is necessary to study other things, to acquire other analytical instruments and to set other standards. Even if one has to do this as an autodidact, it will not be damaging. On the contrary.

I am not ashamed to confess how impoverished my cultural background is. As a result, it does not permit me to write a scholarly essay on the imagination of children, even though it gives me free hand to draw upon my experiences. Nor does it bother me that I must decline to document all that I have said with a comprehensive bibliography, so that everything may seem as though it were improvised or like inventions pulled out of a hat. I am sorry to be ignorant, but I do not regret cutting a poor figure. In fact, I would say that it is necessary to know how to cut a poor figure on certain occasions.

Now, having said all this, I shall admit that I owe a great debt to Umberto Eco's book, *Le forme del contenuto* (*The Forms of the Contents*), especially to his essays "I percorsi del senso" ("The Ways of Meaning") and "Semantica della metafora" ("The Semantics of the Metaphor"). I read them, took notes about them, and forgot them. But I am certain that something of their intellectual brilliance rubbed off on me.

Eco's essay "Generazione di messaggi estetici in una lingua edenica" ("The Generation of Aesthetic Messages in an Edenic Language") serves as a striking example of a tendency in our times to break down the barriers between art and science, mathematics and play, imagination and logical thinking. It is possible to read this essay like a story. It is possible to transform it into a fascinating toy for children. And Eco would not be offended if I advised friends who are elementary school teachers to do this because, after having adequately explored all the possibilities for play (which are many), they should try to introduce this toy into a fifth grade class. Silvio Ceccato has already demonstrated (see *Il maestro inverosimile* [*The Unlikely Teacher*]) that one should not be afraid of talking about "difficult things" with children. In fact, it is much easier to make the mistake of underestimating them than overestimating them.

Thinking in Pairs
(See chapter 3.)

It is interesting to note how Henri Wallon (*Les origines de la pensée chez l'enfant* [*The Origins of the Child's Thought*]) also discovers "pairs of assonance" in his conversations with children. For example, he asks: "What things are hard and tall?" The answer: "A wall." Or: "Why is it dark at night?" The answer: "Because the moon forgot to turn on the light." The cognitive function of rhyme is at the bottom of the pleasure that the children find here, and greater than the simple gratifying effect of the repetition of a sound.

In his essay "On the Semiotics of Art" in *The Systems of Signs and Soviet Structuralism*, Uspenski discusses this theme on the level of artistic creation: "Phonetic affinity obliges the poet to search for semantic connections between the words as well. In this way, phonetics generates the thought."

Estrangement
For the concept of estrangement, see Victor Shklovsky's essays "The Structure of the Novella and the Romance" and "Art as Device" in *The Russian Formalists*: "The purpose of art is to transmit the impression of the object as vision and not as recognition." "The process of art is the process of estranging an object." "In order to make an object into an artistic factor it is necessary to estrange it from the numerous factors of life . . . to shake the object . . . to lift the object from its series of usual associations."

The "Subliminal Perception"
The phonetic attraction between "hung up" (*appeso*) and "turned on" (*acceso*) in chapter 4 could have happened on the unconscious level, on the level that Tauber and Green call the "subliminal perception" in their book *Prelogical Experience*: "People who are extremely creative pick up the material of subliminal perception with great readiness." They provide the example of the German chemist August Kekule, who dreamed one night about a snake with a tail in its mouth and interpreted it as a presentiment of his projects of conceptualizing certain structural problems of chemistry. In short, he dreamed first about a snake eating its tail and then had the idea of "the benzene ring." In reality, the dream work did not *create*—according to the authors—something new. Rather it utilized "subliminal perceptions," verbal or visual, that constituted a mine for the active imagination.

Fantasy and Logical Thinking

With regard to the stories invented by children (see the chapters "The Word *Hi,*" "Light and Shoes," and "Peter and the Putty"), it seems to me that the reflections of John Dewey in *How We Think* are worth considering:

> The imaginative stories poured forth by children possess all degrees of internal congruity; some are disjointed; some are articulated. When connected, they simulate reflective thought; indeed they usually occur in minds of logical capacity. These imaginative enterprises often precede thinking of the close-knit type and prepare the way for it. (p. 5)

"Simulate," "precede," "prepare the way" . . . I don't think it is too arbitrary to deduce from this that if we want to teach people how to *think*, we must first teach them how to *invent*.

Here is another wonderful reflection by Dewey:

> Thought must be reserved for the new, the precarious, the problematic. Hence, the mental constraint, the sense of being lost, that comes to pupils when they are invited to turn their thoughts upon that with which they are already familiar. (pp. 289–90)

Boredom is the enemy of thinking. But if we invite children to think "what would happen if (see chapter 5) everyone in Sicily were to lose their buttons," I would bet all my buttons that they would not bore themselves.

The Riddle as a Form of Cognition

(See chapter 11.)

In Jerome Bruner's *On Knowing: Essays for the Left Hand,* a book that is stimulating for everyone and not just for educators, the author talks about the art and technique of discovery:

> Weldon, the English philosopher, describes problem solving in an interesting and picturesque way. He distinguishes among difficulties, puzzles, and problems. We solve a problem or make a discovery when we impose a puzzle form on a difficulty to convert it into a problem that can be solved in such a way that it gets us where we want to be. That is to say, we recast the difficulty into a form that we know how to work with—then we work it. Much of what we speak of as discovery consists of knowing how to impose a workable kind of form on various kinds of difficulties. A small but crucial part of discovery of the highest order is to invent and develop effective models or "puzzle forms." It is in this area that the truly powerful mind shines. But it is surprising to what degree perfectly ordinary people can, given the benefit of instruction, construct quite interesting and what, a century ago, would have been considered greatly original models. (pp. 94–95)

In his book, *L'educazione della mente* (*The Education of the Mind*), Lucio Lombardo Radice dedicates a fascinating chapter to the riddle "in all its many different forms." In particular he analyzes the "guess-what game," in which one player "thinks" about something (an object, an animal, a person, etc.) and another tries to guess what it is with a series of questions until he or she discovers the answer.

> From the perspective of intellectual maturation and acquisition of a cultural heritage, it is one of the richest and most useful games. To begin with, it is necessary to teach children the method that they are to use to guess (if left to themselves the first time they will not know what to ask). The best method is that of gradually restricting the range of possibilities. Man, woman, child, animal, vegetable, or mineral? If it is a man, is he living? Did he really live long ago, or is he fictitious? If we know him personally, is he young or old, married or single? . . . The method about which we are talking is much more than just a trick for guessing, it is the principal method of the mind: classification, the regrouping of experienced data in concepts. The most interesting questions arise. More and more subtle and precise distinctions are made. An object—was it made by men, or is it a natural object? . . . Et cetera.

The word *riddle* appears curiously in Peter Brown's *Augustine of Hippo*, in the chapter in which the author talks about Augustine as preacher and his way of interpreting the Bible as a coded message, so to speak.

> We shall see that Augustine's attitude toward allegory summed up a whole attitude toward knowledge. But his hearers might have had less sophisticated reasons for enjoying the sermons of their bishop. For, seen in this light, the Bible became a gigantic puzzle—like a vast inscription in unknown characters. It had all the elemental appeal of the riddle: of the most primitive form of triumph over the unknown which consists in finding the familiar beneath an alien guise. (p. 253)

The passage that follows is also interesting:

> The Africans, particularly, had a Baroque love of subtlety. They had always loved playing with words; they excelled in writing elaborate acrostics; *hilaritas*—a mixture of intellectual excitement and sheer aesthetic pleasure at a notable display of it—was an emotion they greatly appreciated. Augustine would give them just this. (p. 254)

I would also like to recommend *La matematica dell'uomo della strada nel problema delle scelte* (*The Mathematics of the Man of the Street in the Problem of Choice*) by Vittorio Checcucci in which he presents his own and his students' research from the seminar of the Institute of Mathematics at the University of Pisa, created in association with a middle school and the Institute for Nautical Science of Livorno. The "primary subject matter" of the research consisted of some riddles and problems that were commonly told in that region: "How does one save cabbages from a goat and a goat from a wolf when all three have to be carried over a bridge separately?"

The Effect of Amplification

The transition from the original fairy tale to the "recast fairy tale" (see chapter 18) is brought about essentially through "amplification" of the type described in the essay with the same title by A. K. Zolkovsky, published in Italy in *I sistemi di segni e lo strutturalismo sovietico*: "An element that is at first fully trivial and insignificant suddenly becomes a decisive factor when placed in a particular context. This becomes possible through the multi-faceted and so-to-speak asymmetrical character of things: what is meaningless in a certain sense prepares the way under certain conditions for something else that is difficult and important." In physics and cybernetics this effect is called amplification: "In the process of amplification, a small quantity of energy, acting as a signal, sets in motion great masses of stored-up energy that are freed and produce effects of great importance." According to Zolkovsky, amplification can be considered as a "structure" of every discovery, whether it be artistic or scientific.

A secondary element of the original fairy tale "liberates" the energy of the new fairy tale by acting as amplifier.

Theater for Children

Regarding development of "theater for children"—that is, ways to produce children's theater within and outside the school—there are several important books other than the one by Franco Passatore and friends cited in chapter 20. See: *Il lavoro teatrale nella scuola* (Florence: La Nuova Italia, 1971); Fiorenzo Alfieri, "Le tecniche del teatro nella pedagogia Freinet" in *Cooperazione educativa* 11-12 (1971); Giuliano Parenti, *Facciamo teatro* (Turin: Paravia, 1971); Sergio Liberovici and Remo Rostagno, *Un paese—Esperienze di drammaturgia infantile* (Florence: La Nuova Italia, 1972); and Guiseppe Bartolucci, ed., *Il teatro dei ragazzi* (Milan: Guaraldi, 1972).

Experts might be tempted to reject the book by Giuliano Parenti because it doesn't deal with children as "producers" or their techniques and experiences. His book is more of a guide to "theater practice," and it does not treat children as creators of their own texts very much. It talks about theater "made" by children, but not really "children's theater" in the genetive sense. Fiorenzo Alfieri's article goes to the other extreme. He examines how children improvise scenes, how they use minimal technical means, recite spontaneously, and involve the spectators, all under the sign of a magnificent "uniqueness that cannot be repeated." Here theater is like a "vital movement," not a scene that is "re-lived."

Personally, I find the "Theater-Play-Life" movement the most significant, but I also think that Parenti's idea of a "Grammar of Theater," which can expand the horizon of the child's creativity, is also extremely important. After the first improvisations it is necessary to enrich them so that the game does not become used up. Freedom needs the support of technique in a difficult but necessary equilibrium. This is also what Schiller said.

I want to add that it would be wonderful if there were also a "theater *for* children" to satisfy other—and no less authentic—cultural needs.

"Children's theater" and "theater for children" are two different things, but they are equally important if both are—and really know how to put themselves—at the service of children.

Fantastic Market Research

A modest treatment of "fantastic market research" (see chapter 23) is contained in my little book, *I viaggi di Giovannino Perdigiorno* (*The Travels of Giovannino Perdigiorno*). The protagonist of this story visits, in succession, men made of sugar, the planet of chocolate, men made out of soap, men made out of ice, men made out of rubber, men made out of clouds, the melancholy planet, the children's planet, the "most" men (strongest, fattest, poorest, et cetera), men made out of paper (lined and graph), men made of tobacco, the country without sleep (where the "rise and shine" song is heard instead of the good-night lullaby), men made out of wind, the country of "nes" (where nobody knows how to say "no" or "yes"), and the country without errors (which does not exist, but perhaps it will one day). I'm not writing about my book to publicize myself, but because many different children, after having looked at the book and read the first few pages, did not even wait for the end, but began immediately inventing countries and men made out of the strangest stuff, out of alabaster, cotton, and even out of electricity. After they had grasped the concept and the project, they began using it in their own way, just as they regularly use their toys. To have generated the desire in children to play seems to me to be a great success for a book.

The Teddy Bear
(See chapter 28.)

There are many convincing essays that explain the presence of stuffed bears, rubber dogs, wooden horses, and other animals in the world of toys. Each toy animal fulfills an emotional function that has already been fully depicted. The child who takes his teddy bear to bed has the right not to know exactly why he is doing this. We know why, more or less. The child receives the warmth and protection of the father and mother who at that moment can no longer reassure him through physical contact. The rocking horse has certainly something to do with the fascination of riding, and with the training to become a soldier, at least in a subliminal way as in the days of antiquity. But in order to explain the entire relationship between the child and the toy animal, it is necessary to go even further back in time. We must return to those distant times when the first animals were domesticated and the first young animals began to live among the tribe and family. The young animals were perfectly suited for growing up with the children. We must go back even further, to the depths of totemism, when not only the child but the entire tribe of hunters elevated an animal to become its protector and benefactor, proclaimed it as the tribal father, and assumed its name.

The first relationship with animals was of a magical nature. The fact that the child can experience this phase again in his development is a theory that circulated some time ago without convincing everyone. But the little teddy bear has something of the totem about it. The domain in which it lives has even the contours of myths, which are not arbitrary creations of the imagination, but forms for approximating reality.

When the child gets bigger, he forgets his teddy bear. But not completely. The patient animal will continue to snuggle within him as in a warm bed, and one fine day it will jump out unexpectedly, unrecognizable at first glance. . . .

Surprisingly, we see this occur in a passage of V. Gordon Childe's book *Man Makes Himself.* The author writes the following, in another context:

> Some degree of abstraction is, however, a feature of any language. But having thus abstracted the idea of the bear from its concrete and actual surroundings and stripped it of many particular attributes, you may combine the idea with other similarly abstracted ideas or endow it with attributes, though you have never encountered a bear in such surroundings or with such attributes. You may, for example, endow your bear with speech, describe him playing a musical instrument. You can play with your words, and that may contribute to

mythology and magic. It may also lead to inventions, if the things you are talking or thinking about can be actually made and tried. Talk of winged men certainly preceded by a long time the invention of a workable flying-machine.

This is a beautiful passage that says more than it seems about the importance of playing with words. And the bear is a perfect fit here. But aren't "primitive" people, who endow the bear with the ability to speak, and children, who have their teddies speak while playing with them, the same people? I suspect that when Gordon Childe was a child he played with a teddy bear, and that the unconscious memory of this influenced the above passage.

A Verb for Playing
(See chapter 30.)

"The children know a form of the past tense more than the grammar," I wrote on January 28, 1961, in an article published in *Paese sera* dedicated to the imperfect tense that children use "when they assume the role of an imaginary figure, when they enter into the fairy tale, exactly when they make the final preparations for their game." This imperfect, the legitimate son of the "once upon a time there was" that provides the beginning of the fairy tale, is actually a special present, an invented time, precisely a verb for playing; for grammar, it is a past present. Dictionaries and grammar books, however, seem to ignore this special use of the imperfect. In his useful *Dizionario grammaticale*, Vincenzo Ceppellini notes five very good ways to use the imperfect, and he defines the fifth as the "classical time in descriptions and fairy tales." But he overlooks the games of children. Alfredo Panzini (see *La parola e la vita* [*The Word and Life*]) comes very close to making the decisive discovery when he says that the imperfect "embraces the suggestive moments of poetical evocations and recollections," and even closer when he notes that *fabula*, from which we obtain *favola* (fairy tale), comes from the Latin *fari*, that is, to speak (*favola*, "the spoken thing"). But neither succeeds in classifying an "imperfect of the fairy tale."

Giacomo Leopardi, who had a truly fabulous ear for verbs, succeeded in picking up in Petrarch an imperfect in the meaning of a past conditional: "*Ch'ogni altra sua voglia / era a me morte, e a lei infamia rea*" ("That every other desire of hers / was death for me, and for her, disgraceful infamy"). That is, it *would have been* death for me. But we see that he did not pay attention to the verbs of children, when he saw them playing and jumping "in a crowd on the little square" and took pleasure, the good man, in their "cheerful noise." And to think that perhaps in that cheerful noise there was also the voice of a little boy who suggested playing a naughty game: "I *was* the humpback, the young count with a humpback. . . ."

In his *Grammatica rivoluzionaria*, Toddi comes up with a fortuitous image along these lines: "The imperfect is often used as background scenery, in front of which the rest of the action develops. . . ." When children say "I was," they shift the background to the front and change the scene. But the grammar books do not take any note of them, except to make life difficult for them at school.

Stories of Mathematics

Next to a "mathematics of stories" (see chapter 34) there are also "stories of mathematics." Whoever follows Martin Gardner's column "Mathematical Games" in the journal *Scientific American* understands right away what I mean. The games that mathematicians invent often assume the character of fictions that are only one step away from narrative invention. Here, for example, is the game of "Life," created by John Norton Conway, a mathematician from Cambridge (*Scientific American*, May 1971). It consists of simulating on the computer the origins, the transformation, and the decline of a society of living organisms. In this game, the initially asymmetrical configurations tend to become symmetrical. Professor Conway calls them "beehive," "light," "pond," "snake," "ferry," "boat," "glider," "clock," "toad," et cetera. He assures us that they constitute "a marvelous show to watch on the computer screen." In the final analysis, it is a show in which the imagination observes itself and its own structures.

In Defense of Puss in Boots

Regarding the child who listens to fairy tales (see chapter 35) and the possible content that a child hears in them, I would like to discuss an article by Sara Melauri Cerrini (in *Giornale dei genitori*, December 1971) about the moral of *Puss in Boots*, in which she states:

> In the stories for children it often happens that someone dies at the beginning and leaves the children with some property and other goods as the inheritance. The least valuable object always has a magical quality to it. In general, the brothers, who are the heirs, do not like one another. The most fortunate one wants to have everything and lets the others fend for themselves. That is the way it is in our story, in which the youngest is the least fortunate. He is left only with a cat and does not know how to keep himself from starving. Fortunately, the cat, who calls him master, places itself voluntarily at his service and promises to help him. This cat is in reality none other than a clever rogue who knows the ways of the world. He also knows that appearances

count, and this is why he uses the few coins that his master gives him to buy a handsome suit, boots, and a cap. Dressed in this manner, and carrying a gaudy present, he appears before the king in order to obtain what he wants. Here a tried and tested technique is already revealed to the children, a technique for moving out from under the shadow, to approach people who hold power, and to make one's fortune: dress yourself nicely, be aware that you have an important mission to fulfill, bring a gift to those whom you want to impress, use an authoritarian manner to intimidate anyone who stands in your way, present yourself in the name of an important person, and the doors of the world will open for you.

And after the entire fairy tale has been recapitulated like this, we have the conclusion:

Here is the moral of the fairy tale: with cunning and deceit, one can become as powerful as a king. Since the family kindness, the mutual aid among the brothers, is lacking, it is necessary to obtain aid from someone who knows the system, that is, from a politician like the cat in order to become a stupid simpleton like the powerful person usually is.

In my commentary (below) on Melauri's interpretation of this old fairy tale, I do not contest its validity, but I do recommend caution. One can demystify things quickly, but one can also miss the target. It is true that in *Puss in Boots* the setting and the costumes are medieval and parallel the theme of cunning as a defense weapon or a weapon of attack by the weak against the powerful. This theme belongs to an ideology of the oppressed and represents the way of life of the serfs, who are capable of conniving (everyone gives a hand in tricking the king), but not of genuine solidarity. However, the cat as such is another matter. . . .

In my "Defense of *Puss in Boots*," I wrote that one would do well not to forget what Propp wrote in his book *The Historical Roots of the Fairy Tale* regarding the motifs of "magic helpers" and "magic gifts," which are among the major motifs in the popular folk tales. According to Propp (and others as well), the animal that figures in the tale as a benefactor of man, or helps him to perform difficult tasks, or rewards him in an extraordinary way for saving it during a hunt is—now dressed as a "worldly" and purely literary figure—the totem-animal venerated by primitive hunting tribes, which had a kind of religious pact with it. During the transition to non-migratory, farming societies, people abandoned the old totem religions, but retained a particular and intense bond with animals.

In the old rites of initiation, the young boys of the tribe were assigned an animal protector, a "guardian spirit." After these rites were abandoned, stories about these "guardian spirits" remained. The animal protector was transformed into the "helpful fairy" in the folk tales and lived on in people's imaginations, acquiring over time different meanings, so that it is difficult to recognize the guardian spirits in the various disguises that they had to wear.

We are obliged to use our imaginations to retrace the path of the fairy tale, to divest it of its lively colors and to reach its most secret core: then we can once again recognize the young initiate in the orphan or in the youngest of the three brothers (for it is always the initiate who is at the center of this type of fairy tale). Then we can also recognize the "guardian spirit" in the cat that takes it upon itself to make fortune shine upon the boy. And if we return to the fairy tale at this point, it can be that the cat suddenly reveals itself to have two faces—one of the initiator who introduces the boy to a corrupt and inhuman world, all perfectly described by Sara Melauri; the other of the ally who seeks justice for his protégé. And in any event, this old cat, heir to obscure traditions that go back thousands of years, a relic of the entombed and silent times of prehistory, appears to be much more respectable than the corrupt rogue or a phony swindler at the king's court.

Naturally, the child who hears the fairy tale about the cat with boots experiences it in a present that has no place for history or prehistory. But in some inexplicable way the child senses perhaps that the genuine core of the fairy tale is not the career of the false Marquis of Carabas, but the relationship between the young man and the cat, between the orphan and the animal. This is perhaps the most durable image—and, on an emotional level, the most effective. This image settles in the child's emotional framework, often partly formed by an animal, real or imaginary (toy), that assumes a role of great importance, already described by psychology. . . .

In issue numbers 3 and 4 (1972) in *Giornale dei genitori*, Laura Conti wrote a new "Defense of *Puss in Boots*," which I shall repeat here almost in its entirety:

I want to tell how I experienced the tale of *Puss in Boots* as a small child almost fifty years ago.

First of all, the cat, just like his little master and me, was somebody little in the world of big people. But his boots placed him in a position to take very big steps—that is, to be able to step out of his condition of smallness and yet remain in it. I, too, wanted *to remain little*, but to do things that big people do, to do battle with them on their own terrain, in a big way. . . .

The relationship of little and big departed from its actual meaning, its dimensions, to project itself figuratively. The cat is not only little, but it is also underestimated, considered useless; its presence in the house became a tedious whim of mine. This is why it pleased me so much that the little useless animal became a powerful ally. The cat's actions did not interest me at all. I forgot all about them: it was necessary to read the *Giornale dei genitori* for me to recall his clever diplomacy, and I confess that his diplomacy was rather vulgar. But for me, the cat's actions were not as important as the results it achieved: it was significant for me that he was able to *win* while betting on the *loser*, if I may be permitted to express the feelings of a child in the language of adults. (In fact, the young man who inherited the cat was pitied at the beginning because of his miserable inheritance.) In short, I was fascinated by the double transformation, from little to big and from loser to winner. I was interested in the victory in and of itself—I was interested in the *improbable* victory. The double nature of the cat (little-big, loser-winner) not only satisfies the paradoxical wish to be big while remaining little, but also the other paradoxical wish, to see the victory of a creature that remains a little, weak, soft cat. I detested the strong in the fairy tale battles between the strong and weak, and I took the side of the weak. But if the weak won, there was the risk that they would have to be considered strong, and one would have to hate them. The story of *Puss in Boots* averted this risk because the cat, even if he wins the game against the king, remains a cat. The key issue here is similar to the situation of David and Goliath, but it is with a David who continues to be a shepherd and never becomes the powerful King David. I am not at all drawing this comparison *a posteriori*: at the same time that I was told the story about *Puss in Boots*, I also heard the biblical story. And the fact that the shepherd became king did not please me. What I liked most was that he killed the giant with his little sling. In contrast to David, the cat defeated the king, but he did not become king. He remained a cat.

Thus, if I think about my personal experience, I can fully confirm everything that you say: it was not the content but the "movement" that was essential in the fairy tale. The content could have been conformist or reactionary, but the movement was very different because it demonstrated that what counts in life is not the friendship of kings but the friendship of cats—that is, the friendship of little creatures, underestimated and weak, who know how to succeed against kings.

Expressive Activity and Scientific Experience

As a commentary on chapter 41 ("Imagination, Creativity, School"), see the following passage from *I modi dell'insegnare* (*The Ways of Teaching*) by Bruno Ciari:

At first glance it would seem that there is no point of contact between expressive activity, creativity, and scientific experience. On the contrary, there is a close relationship. Children who use brushes, paints, paper, and drawing paper to express themselves, who cut out things, paste them, and mold them, develop habits through these activities of making things concrete, adhesive, and exact. These habits contribute to the formation of a general scientific attitude in which a creative aspect is always present anyway, and this aspect reveals itself in the capacity of the real scientist to make use of the most simple means from his immediate surroundings for his experiments. Even though we may all agree that scientific education must have its starting point in facts, observations, and the real experience of the child, I would like to emphasize that the most important expressive activity, the free text, stimulates children to observe reality better, to immerse themselves in experience.

The students of Bruno Ciari bred hamsters, learned how to use the counting system of the Maya in their games, discovered a hypothetical period of time in an experiment in preserving meat in ice, and transformed half the class into an artist's studio. In short, they brought imagination into everything that they did.

Art and Science
(See chapter 41.)

There is a most interesting book about the structural analogy and homology between aesthetic and scientific methodologies: *La scienza e l'arte* (*Science and Art*) edited by Ugo Volli. The general thesis is that "scientific work and artistic work have the same common characteristics in that they portray reality, give it meaning, and transform it. That is, they reduce objects and facts to social meanings. They are both *semiotics of the real.*" The various essays, written by many different authors, move along the traditional boundary between art and science: they seek to negate this boundary, to demonstrate that it is not justified, and to discover a common ground that is becoming larger, where art and science can work with instruments that are becoming more and more similar. For instance, the computer helps the mathematician just as much as it does the artist in the search for new forms. Painters, architects, and scientists work together in centers of automatic production of plastic forms. Nake's formula for his computer graphics would work wonderfully in a grammar of the imagination, and in fact, I shall recopy it here:

> Given a finite repertory of R signs, a finite number of M rules in order to combine these signs with one another, and given a finite intuition I, which determines from case to case which signs and which rules are to be chosen under R and M. The totality of these three elements (R, M, I) will then represent the aesthetic program.

Here it must be emphasized that I represents the intervention of chance. And it can also be observed that the whole thing has the form of a fantastic binominal, in which E and M are the norm and I is creative arbitrariness. "Even in art," the artist Paul Klee had already written in the pre-cybernetics epoch, "there is sufficient space for exact research."

Bibliography

Alfieri, Fiorenzo. "Le tecniche del teatro nella pedagogia Freinet," in *Cooperazione educativa* 11–12 (Florence, 1971).

Arnheim, Rudolf. *Towards a Psychology of Art*. London: Faber, 1967.

Bann, Stephen, and Bowlt, John E., eds. *Russian Formalism: A Collection of Articles and Texts in Translation*. New York: Barnes & Noble, 1973.

Bartolucci, Giuseppe, ed. *Il teatro dei ragazzi*. Milan: Guaraldi, 1972.

Brown, Peter. *Augustine of Hippo*. London: Faber, 1967.

Bruner, Jerome S. *On Knowing: Essays for the Left Hand*. Cambridge, Mass.: Harvard University Press, 1962.

———. *Studies in Cognitive Growth*. New York: Wiley, 1966.

Ceccato, Silvio. *Il maestro inverosimile*. Milan: Bompiani, 1972.

Ceppellini, Vincenzo. *Dizionario per il buon uso della lingua italiana*. Milan: G. Sormani/Novara, 1956.

Checcucci, Vittorio. *Creatività e matematica*. Florence: Libreria editrice fiorentina, 1971.

Childe, V. Gordon. *Man Makes Himself*. London: Watts, 1936.

Ciari, Bruno. *I modi dell'insegnare*. Ed. Alberto Alberti. Rome: Riuniti, 1972.

Civian and Segal. *I sistemi di segno e lo strutturalismo sovietico*. Milan: Bompiani, 1969.

Cropley, John Arthur. *Creativity*. London: Longmans, 1967.

De Bartolomeis, Francesco. *Il bambino dai tre ai sei anni e la nuova scuola infantile*. Florence: La Nuova Italia, 1968.

Dewey, John. *How We Think*. Boston: D. C. Heath, 1910; rev. ed. 1933.

Dolci, Mariano. *I burattini—strumento pedagogico per la scuola*. Reggio Emilia: Assessorato alle istituzioni culturali del Comune di Reggio Emilia, Terno stampa, 1972.

Eco, Umberto. *Le forme del contenuto*. Milan: Bompiani, 1972.

Faeti, Antonio. *Guadare le figure*. Turin: Einaudi, 1972.

Fattori, Marta. *Creatività ed educazione*. Bari: Laterza, 1968.

La Porta, Raffaele. *Il senso del comico nel fanciullo*. Bologna: Malipiero, 1957.

Leopardi, Giacomo. *Zibaldone di pensieri*. 3 vols. Ed. Giuseppe Pacella. Milan: Garzanti, 1991.

———. *Zibaldone: A Selection*. Trans. Martha King and Daniela Bini. New York: Peter Lang, 1992.

Liberovici, Sergio and Remo Rostagno. *Un paese—Esperienze di drammaturgia infantile*. Florence: La Nuova Italia, 1972.

Lodi, Mario. *C'è speranza se questo accade al Vho.* Turin: Einaudi, 1972.

―――. *Il paese sbagliato.* Turin: Einaudi, 1970.

Martinet, André. *Eléments de linguistique générale.* Paris: A. Colin, 1960.

Murphy, Gordon. *An Introduction to Psychology.* New York: Harper, 1951.

Novalis (Friedrich von Hardenberg). *Schriften.* Vol. 1. *Das dichterische Werk.* Eds. Paul Kluckhohn and Richard Samuel. Darmstadt: Wissenschaftliche Buchgesellschaft, 1977.

Panzini, Alfredo. *La parola e la vita.* Milan: Mondadori, 1930.

Parenti, Giuliano. *Facciamo teatro.* Turin: Paravia, 1971.

Passatore, Francesco; de Stefanis, Silvio; Fontana, Ave; and de Lucis, Flavia. *Io ero l'albero (tu il cavallo).* Bologna, 1972.

Propp, Vladimir. *Morphology of the Folk Tale.* Eds. Louis Wagner and Alan Dundes. Trans. Laurence Scott. 2nd rev. ed. Austin: University of Texas Press, 1968.

―――. *Theory and History of Folklore.* Ed. Anatoly Liberman. Trans. Adriadna Y. Martin and Richard P. Martin. Minneapolis: University of Minnesota Press, 1984.

Radice, Lucio Lombardo. *L'educazione della mente.* Rome: Editori Riuniti, 1962.

Read, Herbert. *Education through Art.* London: Faber, 1943.

Ribot, Théodule. *Essai sur l'imagination créatrice.* Paris: F. Alcan, 1908.

Robbe-Grillet, Alain. *Les gommes.* Paris: Minuit, 1953.

Russell, Bertrand. *The Analysis of Mind.* London: Library of Philosophy, 1921.

Sartre, Jean-Paul. *L'imagination.* Paris: F. Alcan, 1936.

Schiller, Friedrich. *On the Aesthetic Education of Man in a Series of Letters.* Trans. Reginald Snell. London: Routledge & Kegan Paul, 1954. First published in 1795 as *Über die aesthetische Erziehung des Menschen in einer Reihe von Briefen.*

Shklovsky, Victor. *I formalisti russi.* Turin: Einaudi, 1968.

Stempel, Hans, and Ripkins, Martin. *Auch Kinder haben Gehemnisse: Kalendergeschichten für nachdenkliche Eltern und neugierige Kinder.* Munich: Ellermann, 1972.

Tauber, Edward, and Green, Maurice. *Prelogical Experience: An Inquiry into Dreams and Other Creative Processes.* New York: Basic Books, 1959.

Thompson, Stith. *The Folktale.* New York: Dryden, 1946.

Toddi (Pseudonym for Piero Silvio Rivetta) *Grammatica rivoluzionaria e ragionata della lingua italiana e di orientamento per lo studio delle lingue straniere.* Rome: S. De Carlo, 1947.

Volli, Ugo, ed. *La scienza e l'arte.* Milan: Mazzotta, 1972.

Vygotsky, L. S. *Thought and Language*. Ed. & trans. Eugenia Hanfmann and Gertrude Vakar. Cambridge, Mass.: MIT Press, 1962.
Wallon, Henri. *Les origines de la pensée chez l'enfant*. Paris: Presses Universitaires de France, 1963.
Zolla, Elemire. *Storia del fantasticare*. Milan: Bompiani, 1973.

Authors Cited

Bontempelli, Massimo (1878–1960). Italian novelist and dramatist. One of the initiators of magic realism. Works: *Il figlio di due madri* (1928), *Gente nel tempo* (1936), *Giro del sole* (1941), *L'amante fedele* (1953).

Calvino, Italo (1923–1985). Italian writer known for his neo-realist novels and stories. He also made an important contribution to Italian folklore by publishing *Fiabe italiane* in 1956, translated into English as *Italian Folktales*. Works: *Il sentiero dei nidi di ragni* (*The Path to the Nest of the Spiders*, 1947), *Ultimo viene il corvo* (*Adam, One Afternoon and Other Stories*, 1949), *Il visconte dimezzato* (*The Cloven Viscount*, 1952), *Il barone rampante* (*The Baron in the Trees*, 1957), *Le città invisibile* (*Invisible Cities*, 1972).

Daudet, Alphonse (1840–1897). French writer of naturalist stories, novels, and plays. Important works: *Lettres de mon moulin* (1869), *La petite chose* (1868), *Tartarin de Tarascon* (1872), *Contes du lundi* (1875), *Jack* (1876). The story, "La Chèvre de M. Séguin," ("The Goat of Signor Séguin") was published in *Lettres de mon moulin*.

Ernst, Max (1891–1975). German-born artist who became a French citizen in 1958. A major surrealist painter, he was the leader of the Cologne Dada Group in 1919 and also created collage novels. Works: *Misfortunes of the Immortals* (1943) and *Beyond Painting* (1948).

Freinet, Célestin (1896–1966). French educator. During the 1930s, he rebelled against conservative educational tradition in France and established his own school that stressed work, cooperation, and democratic decision-making. In 1948 he established the Institut Coopératif de l'Ecole Moderne, and his ideas have had a great impact on educators throughout France. Works: *L'education du travail* (1947), *Essai de psychologie appliquée à l'education* (1951), *Les techniques Freinet dans l'école moderne* (1964), *Pour l'école du peuple* (1969).

Gatto, Alfonso (1909–1976). Italian poet and writer. He wrote "hermetic" works: *Porto ai paesi* (1937), *Il capo sulla neve* (1949), *La forza degli occhi* (1953). In 1938 he founded and edited the review *Campo di Marte*.

Husserl, Edmund (1859–1938). German philosopher. Founder of phenomenology, he began his career in mathematics and then began developing his profound notions of phenomenology. Works: *Ideen zu einer neuen Phämenologue und phämenologischen Philosophie* (1913), *Formale und transcendentale Logik* (1929).

Jakobson, Roman (1896–1982). Russian-born linguist. Perhaps the most important member of the Prague School, he was the principal founder of structural linguistics. Works: *Studies in Child Language and Aphasia* (1941), *Preliminaries to Speech Analysis* (1952), *Fundamentals of Language* (1956), *Child Language* (1968), *The Sound and Shape of Language* (1979).

Klee, Paul (1879–1940). Swiss painter, graphic artist, and art theorist. He was associated with the Blaue Reiter group and other avant-garde movements of the twentieth century. Selected works: *On Modern Art* (1924), *Pedagogical Sketchbooks* (1924), *The Thinking Eye* (1961).

Leopardi, Giacomo (1798–1837). Italian poet and writer. Considered the most outstanding Italian poet of the nineteenth century. Selected works: *Canti* (1816–1836); *Operette morali* (1826–27); and his notebooks entitled *Zibaldone* (1817–1837). This title means hodgepodge or compendium— part diary and part notebook for ideas he wanted to develop, in prose and poetry.

Magalotti, Lorenzo (1637–1712). Italian scholar who wrote on a vast number of topics. Works: *Saggi di naturali esperienze* (1667); *Lettere contro gli atei* (1719).

Manzoni, Alessandro (1785–1873). Italian novelist, poet, and politician. Influenced by Sir Walter Scott, he published the influential historical romance *I promessi sposi* (*The Betrothed*) in 1825–26. Other important works: *Il Conte di Carmagnola* (1816–20), *Adelchi* (1822), and *Cinque maggio* (1821).

Montale, Eugenio (1896–1981). Considered by some to be the most important Italian poet of the twentieth century, he received the Nobel Prize for literature in 1975. Works: *Ossi di seppia* (1925), *Le occasioni* (1939), *La bufera e altro* (1956), *Satura* (1971), *Quaderno di quattro anni* (1977), *L'opera in versi* (1980).

Palazzeschi, Aldo (pseudonym for Aldo Giurlani, 1884–1974). Italian poet and writer who belonged to the futurist movement. Poetry: *Poesie* (1930). Prose: *Il codice di Perela* (1911), *Le sorelle Materassi* (1934), *Il palio dei buffi* (1936).

Sbarbaro, Camillo (1888–1967). Italian poet and writer. Poetry: *Pianissimo* (1914), *Rimanenze* (1955), *Primizie* (1958). Prose: *Trucioli* (1920), *Liquidazione* (1928), *Fuochifatui* (1956).

Selected Bibliography of Works by Gianni Rodari

Primary Works

Il libro delle filastrocche. Rome: Edizioni del Pioniere, 1950.

Il manuale del pioniere. Rome: Edizioni di Cultura sociale, 1951.

Il romanzo di Cipollino. Rome: Edizioni di Cultura sociale, 1951. (After 1957: *Le avventure di Cipollino*. Rome: Editori Riuniti.)

Il treno delle filastrocche. Rome: Edizioni di Cultura sociale, 1952.

Le carte parlanti. Florence: Edizioni Toscana Nuova, 1952.

La Freccia azzurra. Florence: CDS, 1953.

Una scuola grande come il mondo. Florence: Potente, 1956.

Gelsomino nel paese dei bugiardi. Rome: Editori Riuniti, 1958.

Filastrocche in cielo e in terra. Turin: Einaudi, 1960.

Favole al telefono. Turin: Einaudi, 1962.

Gip nel televisore. Milan: Mursia, 1962.

Il pianeta degli alberi di Natale. Turin: Einaudi, 1962.

Ai ragazzi, in *Enciclopedia della fiaba*. Roma: Editori Riuniti, 1963.

Castello di carte. Milan: Mursia, 1963.

Il libro degli errori. Turin: Einaudi, 1964.

"Come è nato il libro degli errori" in *Noi Donne* (14 november 1964).

La torta in cielo. Turin: Einaudi, 1966.

"Scuola e civiltà" in A. Bernardini, *Un anno a Pietralata.* Florence: La Nuova Italia, 1968.

"Pinocchio per adulti" in *Paese sera-Libri* (29 September 1968).

Venti storie più una. Rome: Editori Riuniti, 1969.

"Presentazione" in H. C. Andersen, *Fiabe.* Turin: Einaudi, 1970.

"Un amico, un maestro" in *Giornale dei genitori* 10/11 (1970).

"Vita con l'adolescente" in *Giornale dei genitori* 5 (1970).

Le filastrocche del cavallo parlante. Milan: Emme Edizioni, 1970.

Tante storie per giocare. Rome: Editori Riuniti, 1971.

"Discorso pronunciato all'atto di ricevere il premio Andersen" in *Schedario* (January–February, 1971)

"Bruno Ciari e la nascita di una pedagogia popolare in Italia" in *Bruno Ciari e la nascita du una pedagogia popolare in Italia.* Rome: Centro B. Ciari, 1971.

"Presentazione" in *Voglia di scrivere.* Florence: Libreria Editrice Fiorentina, 1971.

Gli affari del Signor Gatto. Turin: Einaudi, 1972.

I viaggi di Giovannino Perdigiorno. Turin: Einaudi, 1972.

Grammatica della fantasia: Introduzione all'arte di inventare storie. Turin: Einaudi, 1973.

Novelle fatte a macchina. Turin: Einaudi, 1973.

"Piccola storia del' limografo" in *Paesa sera* (2 March 1973).

"Per la ricostruzione della scuola di base" in *Giornale dei genitori* 6/7 (1973).

"Pinocchio nella letteratura per l'infanzia" in *Studi collodiani.* Brescia: Fondanzione Collodi, 1976.

Marionette in libertà. Turin: Einaudi, 1974.

La filastrocca di Pinocchio. Rome: Editori Riuniti, 1974.

C'era due volte il barone Lamberto. Turin: Einaudi, 1978.

La gondola fantasma. Turin: Einaudi, 1978.

Parole per giocare. Florence: Manzuoli, 1979.

Bàmbolik. Milan: La Sorgente, 1979.

Il gioco dei quattro cantoni. Turin: Einaudi 1980.

Il cane di Magonza. Ed. Carmine de Luca. Rome: Editori Riuniti, 1982.

Scuola di fantasia. Ed. Carmine de Luca. Rome: Editori Riuniti, 1992.

I cinque libri: Storie fantastiche, favole, filastrocche. Ed. Piono Boero. Turin: Einaudi, 1993.

Secondary Literature

Argilli, Marcello. *Gianni Rodari: Una biografia.* Turin: Einaudi, 1990.

Argilli, Marcello; del Cornó, Lucio; and de Luca, Carmine, eds. *Le provocazioni della fantasia. Gianni Rodari scrittore e educatore.* Rome: Editori Riuniti, 1993.

Bini, G., ed. *Leggere Rodari.* Pavia: Amministrazione Provinciale di Pavia-Ufficio Scuola, 1981.

Cambi, Franco. *Collodi, De Amicis, Rodari: Tre immagini d'infanzia.* Bari: Dedalo, 1985.

———. *Rodari pedagogista.* Rome: Editori Riuniti, 1990.

De Luca, Carmine, ed. *Se la fantasia cavalca con la ragione: Prolungamenti degli itinerari suggeriti dall'opera di Gianni Rodari.* Bergamo: Juvenilia, 1983.

———. *Gianni Rodari: La gaia scienza della fantasia.* Catanzaro: Abramo, 1991.

Petrini, Enzo; Argilli, Marcello; and Bonardi, Carlo, eds. *Gianni Rodari.* Florence: Giunti Marzocco, 1981.

Books in English

Telephone Tales. Trans. Patrick Creagh. London: Harrap, 1965. A selection from *Favole al telefono.*

The Befana's Toyshop: A Twelfth Night Tale. Trans. Patrick Creagh. London: Dent, 1970. Translation of *La freccia azzurra.*

A Pie in the Sky. London: Dent, 1971. Translation of *La torta in cielo.*

Tales Told by a Machine. London: Abelard and Shulman, 1976. A selection from *Novelle fatte a macchina.*

OTHER T&W BOOKS YOU MIGHT ENJOY

Educating the Imagination, Vols. 1 & 2, edited by Christopher Edgar and Ron Padgett. A big selection of the best articles from 17 years of *Teachers & Writers* magazine, with ideas and assignments for writing poetry, fiction, plays, history, folklore, parodies, and much more.

When Stories Come to School: Telling, Writing, & Performing Stories in the Early Childhood Classroom by Patsy Cooper. "A candid and in-depth discussion"—*Creative Classroom.* "A wonderfully personal narrative"—Vivian Gussin Paley. "A very useful sourcebook"—*Kliatt.*

Making Theater by Herbert Kohl tells how to explore improvisation with young people, adapt plays and stories for performance, and much more."Kohl writes with humor, sensitivity, and dedication to the challenge of making theater that exists for the sake of the children who are part of it"—*Portfolio* (Harvard University).

Personal Fiction Writing by Meredith Sue Willis. A complete and practical guide for teachers of writing from elementary through college level. Contains more than 340 writing ideas. "A terrific resource for the classroom teacher as well as the novice writer"—*Harvard Educational Review.*

Blazing Pencils: A Guide to Writing Fiction & Essays by Meredith Sue Willis. Particularly good for middle school students. "Can be used by students themselves or by teachers . . . a fine balance between text, exercises, and examples"—*Kliatt.*

Old Faithful: 18 Writers Present Their Favorite Writing Assignments, edited by Christopher Edgar and Ron Padgett. A collection of sure-fire exercises in imaginative writing for all levels, developed and tested by veteran writing teachers.

The Teachers & Writers Handbook of Poetic Forms, edited by Ron Padgett. This T&W bestseller includes 74 entries on traditional and modern poetic forms by 19 poet-teachers. "A treasure"—*Kliatt.* "The definitions not only inform, they often provoke and inspire. A small wonder!"—*Poetry Project Newsletter.* "An entertaining reference work"—*Teaching English in the Two-Year College.* "A solid beginning reference source"—*Choice.*

The Adventures of Dr. Alphabet by Dave Morice presents 104 amusing and imaginative poetry writing methods that have excited his students for two decades. "Teachers and parents will treasure this collection"—*School Enrichment Model Network News.*

Poetry Everywhere: Teaching Poetry Writing in School and in the Community by Jack Collom & Sheryl Noethe. This big and "tremendously valuable resource work for teachers" (*Kliatt*) at all levels contains 60 writing exercises, extensive commentary, and 450 examples.

•

For a complete free T&W publications catalogue, contact
Teachers & Writers Collaborative
5 Union Square West, New York, NY 10003–3306
(212) 691-6590.